WHAT IF WE DID FOLLOW JESUS?

Melvin E. Schoonover

WHAT IF WE DID FOLLOW JESUS?

Challenges From His Ministry in Town and City

Judson Press ® Valley Forge

**LAKE
VIEW
BOOKS**

Lake View Books are books of outstanding merit and broad interest which originated at the American Baptist Assembly, Green Lake, Wisconsin. The material on which this book is based was presented under the Boardman Lectureship at Green Lake.

WHAT IF WE DID FOLLOW JESUS?

Copyright © 1978
Judson Press, Valley Forge, PA 19481

Unless otherwise indicated, Bible quotations in this volume are in accordance with *The New English Bible,* Copyright © The Delegates of the Oxford University Press and The Syndics of the Cambridge University Press, 1961, 1970.

Other versions of the Bible quoted in this book are:

The Holy Bible, King James Version.

The Bible: A New Translation, Copyright © 1954 by James Moffatt, by permission of Harper & Row, Publishers, Inc.

Revised Standard Version, Copyright © 1946, 1952, 1971, 1973, by the Division of Christian Education of the National Council of the Churches of Christ in the United States of America.

Library of Congress Cataloging in Publication Data

Schoonover, Melvin E.
    What if we did follow Jesus?

    Includes bibliographical references.
    1. Jesus Christ—Person and offices—Addresses, essays, lectures. 2. Christian life—1960—
Addresses, essays, lectures. I. Title.
BT202.S364   232   78-2594
ISBN 0-8170-0791-1

The name JUDSON PRESS is registered as a trademark in the U.S. Patent Office. Printed in the U.S.A.

To the students of
New York Theological Seminary

Introduction

As I am writing this, I am living on the eighteenth floor of an apartment building in New York City, that has 125 families—at least 500 people. This is but one of fourteen buildings in a housing project with more than 1,600 apartments—or a total population of more than 6,000 men, women, and children on a plot of ground not much bigger than the area occupied by one house, a barn, a crib, a hen house, and a milk shed on the farm on which I was born in Indiana.

From the windows of my apartment, I can see two rivers spanned by great bridges. Below me, on pockmarked Second Avenue where a subway lies unfinished because of our infamous financial crisis, day and night there is a steady stream of traffic; and the sound of that traffic, frequently pierced by the sirens of a variety of emergency vehicles, is so familiar as to go generally unnoticed.

My barber is Italian; my doctor, Jewish. The man who cleans my clothes is black, the cashier at the local supermarket is Puerto Rican, and the couple who sold me lettuce and tomatoes from their produce stand for our last dinner party are Korean.

To the southwest of my housing complex is an area of incredible wealth, where limousines draw up at beautifully kept buildings and where smiling, uniformed attendants open the doors for you and others whisk you to luxurious living spaces overlooking the Vanderbilt flower gardens in Central Park.

In every other direction, virtually all one sees from my apartment windows are what people casually call "the slums"—acre after acre of crumbling tenements, interrupted by vacant lots strewn with rubbish and, here and there, a public building with graffiti-scrawled walls. It is an area, despite our declining population, of incredible congestion and almost universal poverty.

This is but one of hundreds of "communities" in the city of New York. This city is my "parish"—this is the setting for my ministry on behalf of and in the name of Jesus the Christ. It is inevitable that I consider that ministry—Jesus' ministry—from an urban perspective. These reflections on the ministry of Jesus make two assumptions. The first is that, whatever the immediate environment in which we work and dwell, all our lives are strongly influenced if not shaped by one pervasive urban culture. Life in a tiny town in the Midwest is only relatively different from life in a big city. The second assumption is that, whatever the immediate environment in which we work and dwell, those who seek to follow Jesus in faith and hope are engaged in one ministry of reconciliation and healing. The locations may be different and the circumstances may vary, yet "there is one body and one Spirit . . . one Lord, one faith, one baptism; one God and Father of all . . ." (Ephesians 4:4-6).

What I have done is to examine Jesus' ministry by examining events in that ministry identified with cities of his day. While I was taught in seminary that Jesus' ministry was shaped by a predominantly rural, agrarian understanding of life, I no longer fully believe it. My own study of Scripture leads me to observe that a great deal of that ministry was conducted in cities and—I believe—shaped by city realities. While they were minuscule in comparison with today's great urban areas, the cities of Jesus' time nevertheless were tremendously influential. They were centers of trade and culture, of political intrigue and creative expression, even as ours are.

This book grew out of a series of lectures given at the National Bible Conference at the American Baptist Assembly, Green Lake, Wisconsin, in July, 1977. The lectures were given in the name of

George Dana Boardman, for thirty years a pastor of the First Baptist Church of Philadelphia and throughout his life preoccupied with the application of the gospel of Christ to social and political issues.

The intent of the lectures overall was to help hearers master five key "events" in Jesus' ministry identified with particular cities. Methodologically, this was facilitated by first putting the event in a geographical, social, and political context. Then a volunteer from the audience read the pertinent Scripture. The lecture next addressed itself to a detailed exegesis of the Bible passage so that—in a sense—the "story" was retold. After probing the story for implications for our ministry and raising one "what if . . . ?" question for people to ponder, I ended each lecture by retelling the Bible event in my own words. Each story (with the exception of the last, which was handled differently), then, was "experienced" in three different forms. The same format has been used here, although admittedly it works better orally than in print.

As always, the questions and discussion that grew out of the presentations were very helpful and illuminating. Some resulted in revisions in the original text. Throughout, a good spirit prevailed. Even when people strongly disagree with some of my conclusions, I felt they exhibited great care and integrity in understanding and sharpening the issues. I am deeply grateful for the sense of community which emerged from our week together.

An unanticipated element of drama was the news of the occurrence, early in the series, of New York's twenty-five hour total power failure and the rioting and looting which took place in many poverty-stricken neighborhoods, including my own—East Harlem. This urban event lent to the lectures an immediacy and, I trust, pertinency which might otherwise have been absent.

Finally, some words of appreciation are due to family and colleagues who made the series "happen." I am grateful to Bill Weisenbach for proposing that I focus on specific cities. Tom Boomershine and Willis Elliott, both formidable scholars of Scripture, were enormously helpful in pointing me to useful sources of information and interpretation. Bill Webber was greatly supportive both in encouraging me to accept the invitation and in enabling me to free up time to prepare.

Margaret Rathnum sent me off to Green Lake with one neatly

typed lecture, and Diana and Polly Schoonover took the yellow, handwritten sheets "hot" from my pen and transcribed them so that each day there was something for me to read other than my own sometimes nearly illegible penmanship. To all these members of my nuclear and professional families, I give hearty thanks.

Contents

Chapters

1 Caesarea Philippi: Who Am I?

               Who Are You? **13**

2 Capernaum: Human Hungers **27**

3 Nazareth and Tyre: Who Belongs? **45**

4 Jericho: The Poor **59**

5 Jerusalem: Politics **71**

Notes **87**

1

Caesarea Philippi: Who Am I? Who Are You?

Two things had taken me to the street that hot summer night. One was fatigued restlessness following a long drive through a series of mountain passes; the other was that my wife had a headache and asked me to try to find her something to relieve it.

"Come here!" was the peremptory invitation. Hesitantly I moved toward them, fearful, yet angry at myself for being fearful. This was, after all, Cortez, Colorado, not New York!

They were both middle-aged men, "native Americans" as they are now sometimes called. One stood—rather unsteadily it seemed to me. The other sat, as I did, in a wheel chair. A large, empty bottle on the ground between them suggested how they had spent their evening.

"Hello, I'm Mel Schoonover," I said, extending my hand to my counterpart. He shook my hand. "Who are you?" I asked.

He replied, "I'm only a drunken Indian."

"You must have a name," I persisted. So, then, I learned he was Miles. He had been crippled fighting in the Korean War, although my cursory examination suggested he had fought many other battles as well and had not always won.

He spoke dreamily of New York and of the "good times" he had had there—although it seemed that New Jersey ports were what he really meant.

I moved to leave. "Don't go," he said.

"I must."

"Okay, take it easy." I returned to my motel.

This hardly seems a very dramatic event. "I am *only* a drunken Indian," he had said. That simple statement has haunted me ever since, raising as it does the whole issue of personal identity in our world. It happened in Cortez, Colorado; but it was the same issue that Jesus dealt with nearly two thousand years ago in another city, Caesarea Philippi.

Caesarea Philippi was an ancient city, strategically located at one of the sources of the Jordan River and heavily fortified to protect the trade routes that went through it. Both its elevation (1,150 feet above sea level) and setting (a fertile plateau marked by luxuriant vegetation and dominated, to the northeast, by the snow-capped bulk of Mount Hermon) made it a desirable place to live. It would have been a particularly attractive place in summer, far cooler than the plain below.

Some scholars say that the Phoenicians had worshiped one of the forms of Baal here; indeed, a few specifically identify it with the town of Baal-gad mentioned in the Book of Joshua. The Greeks, Josephus tells us, made it a center of worship for the god Pan—inscriptions on the cliff and in the caves and grottoes confirm this; and ancient coins suggest that even after its name had been changed to Caesarea, the name Paneas continued to be used.

When Roman Emperor Augustus gave the city to Herod the Great in 20 B.C., in gratitude Herod built a temple of white marble in honor of his benefactor. His son, Philip, went further: he rebuilt and enlarged the city, beautifying it still more, and then named it Caesarea in honor of Tiberias, then the Roman emperor. Since there already was a Caesarea on the Mediterranean, Philip "modestly" sought to distinguish it by adding his own name to the title of his ruler—hence Caesarea Philippi. One authority says that, in the rebuilding of the town, concrete was used for the first time.

In the time of Jesus, Caesarea Philippi was inhabited largely by Gentiles. (An old commentary ominously—and delightfully—says,

"The sinister shadow of Herodian Romanism was over the place"!¹)
Some commentators have assumed that Jesus made use of the town
both because it would be a more pleasant physical setting for personal
meditation and instruction of his disciples and because he would be
unbothered by the crowds which followed him closely everywhere
else. He might even have felt safer here; Herod Antipas was obsessed
with the notion that Jesus was the reincarnation of John the Baptist
and, hence, might be expected to lash out again in murderous fear.
Philip, on the other hand, was seen to be a comparatively sane and
just ruler.

One might further speculate that the choice of Caesarea Philippi
as one center of activity for Jesus and his friends was deliberate,
intended for symbolic value. The place where the king was
inaugurated was apparently very important to the Jews: witness the
significance of Gilgal in relation to Saul and Jerusalem in relation to
David. Let us remember where we are—in an ancient military and
commercial center with a history of affirming various deities,
populated and politically controlled by people whom conservative
Jews would see as enemies. Here a crucial event in the ministry of
Jesus takes place—an event which establishes his identity and ours.

> When he came to the territory of Caesarea Philippi, Jesus
> asked his disciples, "Who do men say that the Son of Man is?"
> They answered, "Some say John the Baptist, others Elijah,
> others Jeremiah, or one of the prophets." "And you," he asked,
> "who do you say I am?" Simon Peter answered: "You are the
> Messiah, the Son of the living God." Then Jesus said: "Simon
> son of Jonah, you are favoured indeed! You did not learn that
> from mortal man; it was revealed to you by my heavenly Father.
> And I say this to you: You are Peter, the Rock; and on this rock I
> will build my church, and the powers of death shall never
> conquer it. I will give you the keys of the kingdom of Heaven;
> what you forbid on earth shall be forbidden in heaven, and what
> you allow on earth shall be allowed in heaven." He then gave his
> disciples strict orders not to tell anyone that he was the Messiah.
> From that time Jesus began to make it clear to his disciples
> that he had to go to Jerusalem, and there to suffer much from the
> elders, chief priests, and doctors of the law; to be put to death
> and to be raised again on the third day. At this Peter took him by

the arm and began to rebuke him: "Heaven forbid!" he said. "No, Lord, this shall never happen to you." Then Jesus turned and said to Peter, "Away with you, Satan; you are a stumbling-block to me. You think as men think, not as God thinks" (Matthew 16:13-23).

Jesus and his closest friends are together in Caesarea Philippi. He engages them in probing conversation. *I know you listen to the gossip and speculations of the people,* he says in effect. *Tell me, what do they say about me? Who do they say I am?*

Indeed there was much for people to talk about. If we follow Matthew's chronology, there had already been Jesus' dramatic baptism, his struggles of body and spirit in the wilderness, and his recruitment of a very mixed bag of disciples. Throughout Galilee and beyond he had established himself as a compelling preacher (witness the so-called Sermon on the Mount proclaiming, among other things, a revolutionary life-style) and also as a teacher and healer of great power.

Already, in the healing of the paralytic, Jesus had become controversial among the religious authorities because he had told the man his sins were forgiven. Only God could do that, the critics said. In preparing his followers to go out to spread the "good news" of the kingdom of heaven, Jesus had told them to go without any kind of defense save that afforded by God's power even though, realistically, they were like sheep going into the presence of wolves. Lest people understand his words and deeds solely in terms of healing and reconciliation, Jesus pointedly said that he had come not to bring peace but a sword—a sword that would cut through all the sham and hypocrisy, selfishness and greed, injustice and human exploitation that characterize those who love themselves more than God.

As time went on, the controversy had heightened. Jesus' enemies sought every opportunity to entrap him in admissions they could label blasphemous or seditious. Fearing for his life, if not his sanity, his family had come to take him home; and, perhaps overcome with grief tinged with bitterness, he had said that his real family were those who did his heavenly Father's will. One who clearly qualified on those grounds was John who had baptized him and who, languishing in Herod's prison because of his condemnation of the king's immorality, now had been executed because of the queen's malice. In sorrow

Jesus hid himself to mourn the passing of still another prophet of Israel. The ever-curious, ever-demanding, ever-needy "crowd," nonetheless, found his hiding place. "His heart went out to them," as *The New English Bible* puts it; and, to the expected ministries of teaching and healing, he now had added that of the miraculous feeding of thousands of people.

Now he comes to Caesarea Philippi. *Who do people say the Son of Man is?* he asks. No one really knows if this is intended by Jesus to be a title for the Messiah. Argyle, in the recent *Cambridge Bible Commentary,* suggests that it may simply represent an Aramaism which means "I."[2] *Who do people say I am?* Perhaps the disciples are embarrassed, as people often are when confronted with their enjoyment of gossip. Yet several of them respond.

Who do people say I am? One response is, "John the Baptist." The reappearance of dead heroes is a familiar theme in contemporary Jewish thought. We have already noted that Herod superstitiously considered Jesus the reincarnation of John the Baptist. So, apparently, did other people. John was a very significant figure of the time. This stern, austere, ascetic man had captured the imaginations and stirred the consciences of people in a way that had not been seen in Israel for a long time. Reeling from decades, even centuries, of political oppression aggravated by a religious establishment seen to be corrupt at worst and insensitive at best, people longed for deliverance. Elaborate traditions had grown up about characteristics of that deliverer. The Messiah, as he was called, the ideal king for a restored Israel, would—among other things—be a friend of the poor and would, through authoritative teaching of the Torah (the Law), bring about the cleansing of religious practices. This king would reign in righteousness and justice. So desperate for his coming were the people that they had so hailed John, but he had cried out, *No, no, I am not he. I prepare the way for one far greater than I.* By his courage and integrity, John had aroused the hopes of the people that the Messiah would come soon.

Who do people say I am? Jesus asks; and the disciples respond, "Some say John the Baptist."

There are other opinions as well. *Who do people say I am?* Another response is, "Elijah," the greatest of the ancient prophets. Elijah had dedicated himself to extirpating the worship of heathen gods from

Israel's life and to raising the ethical level of Israel's religious faith. Elijah, according to the prophet Malachi, would return just before the fearsome Day of Judgment. Ecclesiasticus, an apocryphal writer, said the prophet would come to "restore the tribes" of Israel. Elijah was seen in the traditions of Jesus' day as the herald of the Messiah and by the early church as indeed having come in the figure of John the Baptist. Elijah appeared at the Transfiguration as the representative of Old Testament prophecy in the confirmation of Jesus' kingship. *Who do people say I am?* Jesus asks, and the disciples respond, *Some say you are Elijah.*

There are still more opinions. *Who do people say I am?* Another response is Jeremiah. Only Matthew's account includes him; yet it seems appropriate, for Jeremiah was greatly venerated among the Jews. They had legends that when the temple was destroyed Jeremiah hid the tabernacle, the ark, and the altar of incense in a cave on Mount Pisgah and had vowed that one day they would be restored; a very late Jewish writer said that Jeremiah himself would appear to restore these sacred objects. Another legend told of his appearing to Judas Maccabaeus during a previous period of great unrest in the history of the Jews and encouraging him to fight on. Jeremiah was, in the experience of Israel, if we may borrow Mohammed Ali's favorite description of himself, "the greatest," and it would have been deemed a great honor to have one's name and reputation linked with the prophet.

Indeed, as the *Abingdon Bible Commentary* puts it, the prophets with which people associated Jesus "were men of fearless courage, singular devotion, unflinching loyalty to high ideals, and men of great simplicity and stern self-discipline."[3] Jesus had claimed the title of prophet for himself at the time when his credentials had been attacked by the people of Nazareth who sought to dismiss him with the phrase, *Is he not the carpenter's son?* The disciples now confirm his right to the title of prophet.

Who do people say I am? Jesus asks; the disciples respond, *Some say Jeremiah or one of the prophets.*

It is interesting to note that, apparently, it did not occur to anyone to say that Jesus was Jesus himself in all *his* uniqueness.

Even that does not end the interrogation, however. Jesus has another question. "And you," he asks, "who do you say I am?" There is less eagerness to respond now. It is easier, safer, to confine oneself to reporting the opinions of others. Some commentators speak of Simon Peter as "spokesman" for the group, and in one way he is, for he speaks what they all believe—even if they are reluctant to say it out loud. There is no indication there was a caucus and that Peter was selected to speak on their behalf. In his customary rash, uncalculating fashion, he says what is on *his* mind. Yet it is both the collective affirmation and a very personal confession: "You are the Messiah, the Son of the living God."

One cannot help wondering if this might not have been the confirmation Jesus had been looking for—clarification of his own questions and uncertainties. "Flesh and blood"—that is, all the intelligence and cunning of humanity—has not been the source of this confession. Instead God revealed it to Simon Peter, Jesus says, and that means Peter has been specially favored by God.

That alone was the reason he could make such a bold statement. We can hardly imagine the courage Peter's profession took; we take for granted that *everyone* knows Jesus is the Messiah. Yet it would have been considered scandalous for Peter to say this. Israel had so often been disappointed; their history knew many charlatans, many pretenders to the throne of David which tradition held would one day be occupied by the Messiah. So the pressures would have been great and anyone bold enough to affirm Jesus as Messiah would certainly have experienced ridicule, derision, and hostility. The intensity of social pressure was comparable, I suspect, to that now being experienced by the followers of Sun Myung Moon.

So this makes it all the more understandable why Jesus gives Peter a new name: henceforth he is to be known as "the Rock." To be sure, this is a play on words with his name—Peter (in Greek, *Petros* means Peter; *petra* means "rock"). It is more than that, however. It is the recognition that Peter is made of sterner stuff than hitherto suspected. There is an integrity to him, despite his obvious frailty, which justifies making his nickname his real name.

Therefore, Jesus says, *On that unlikely and unexpected foundation, stonelike in character, I will build my church; and the powers of hell will never overwhelm it. There will always be another "Peter" to take the place of the first one, and another, and another.*

It is interesting to note that in his prophecy Isaiah termed Abraham also to be a "rock" (Isaiah 51:1-2). The midrash—a traditional Jewish commentary on the Old Testament—says: "God is like unto a king who wished to build himself a house. He digged and digged, but in each place water sprang up and destroyed the foundation he had dug. At last he chanced to dig where deep down he came upon a rock; then said he, 'Here will I build.' In like manner God, wishing to create the world, looked out upon the generations of Enoch that would be, and that of the flood, and said, 'How can I make a world out of such sinners, who will people it with those who will annoy me?' But when he saw Abraham he said, 'Oh, here is the rock upon whom I can found a world.'"[4]

To Peter are entrusted the "keys of the kingdom"—he is like the king's steward, possessing access to all the treasures of his lord; and his heavenly Lord will confirm whatever his decisions may be—what he permits will be permitted, what he forbids will be forbidden. By his choices, to use expressions somewhat familiar to church folk, Peter will "loose" or "bind" many things in relation to the people who share his faith in Jesus as Messiah.

What troublous and troublesome teaching for us Protestants! Does it mean that Peter was special? Of course! One cannot escape that conclusion from reading the New Testament. Even as portrayed in the Gospels and Acts, Peter had a role of leadership in the early church that was responsible and important. At the same time it is clear that there were other leaders—James, John, Paul, to name the three most obvious. The Roman Catholic Church has sought to confine Peter's "power" to those who followed him, as they claim, in a particular office. That still does not ring true to this story, even in a time when—God be praised—it has become almost natural for Baptists to say nice things about Catholics! It was Peter's faith, Peter's commitment, Peter's daring which were the rock upon which the church is built; and the church is sustained through the ages by the same kind of faith, commitment, and daring, even though these qualities are attached to many other names.

What a risk God continues to take! I have a fantasy of waking up some day to find the skyscrapers of Manhattan slowly sinking into the ocean. (Indeed there are those who predict that it will inevitably happen to the banks and stock exchanges of the lower end of the island!) Why doesn't it happen? Only because the buildings are built on solid rock. Providing secure foundations for multistory buildings in New York is often the most costly part of the entire project, for sometimes the rock is much farther beneath the surface than one assumes.

How risky to build a community of faith on human beings! Hardly has the astonishment around Peter's recognition of Jesus as Messiah subsided when he is in disagreement with his Lord. From that time Jesus spells out in very precise terms what lies before him—he will go to Jerusalem once more, be persecuted by the authorities, be put to death, and finally "on the third day" be raised from the dead. Peter is scandalized—and it is clear from the total story that once again he speaks the mind of the others—that the Messiah should suffer and die. Nothing in the messianic traditions prepared them for this; the Suffering Servant of Isaiah was not a messianic figure for them at this point. Peter vehemently objects to this "nonsense" and loudly proclaims that it will never be allowed. After all, he has been led to his confession that Jesus is the Messiah because of his perception that the Lord has absolute power over evil. The episode ends with Jesus' angry rebuke: *Get away from me . . . Satan . . . stumbling block, not rock. . . .* He who just minutes before had been hailed for being favored by God with the revelation of wondrous truth is now denounced for thinking "as men think." What a risk God takes when he builds his church on the faith of human beings!

There is one more thing to note about the story. After Peter's confession and before their quarrel, Jesus commands the disciples, *Don't tell anyone.* Is this because Jesus knows that people, including the authorities, will continue to misunderstand the nature of the kingdom he is instituting? James Barr postulates that Jesus' reticence had nothing to do with desire to avoid worldly political and nationalistic associations of the popular messianic concepts of his time. Instead Jesus sought to challenge people "with the enigma of His person and deeds; only by trusting in Him do [people] know who He is."[5]

This calls to memory the moving concluding paragraph of Albert Schweitzer's *The Quest of the Historical Jesus:*

> He comes to us as One unknown, without a name, as of old, by the lake-side, He came to those men who knew Him not. He speaks to us the same word: "Follow thou me!" and sets us to the tasks which He has to

fulfil for our time. He commands. And to those who obey Him, whether they be wise or simple, He will reveal Himself in the toils, the conflicts, the sufferings which they shall pass through in His fellowship, and, as an ineffable mystery, they shall learn in their own experience Who He is.[6]

I still vividly remember the shock on the suburban woman's face when she heard my answer to her question. The question was, "What is the most serious problem people in your parish face?" She doubtless thought I would cite drug addiction or poor housing or poverty. She clearly was not prepared for the answer: "Personal identity."

"But that," she expostulated, "is *our* chief problem!"

"Who am I?" It is a question Dietrich Bonhoeffer asked in prison. It is a question I hear from "all sorts and conditions of men," as the old Episcopal prayer book put it—the adolescent, the widow, the clergy. We are all part of a society which exerts almost irresistible pressure to make us a number, a function, or a category. Our identity, then, becomes a green, plastic American Express card (gold, if our credit rating is especially good!) or a title or a description.

Here are two personal illustrations. A few years back I was riding up in an elevator with the somewhat pretentious editor of a law journal. Someone he knew joined us. "Have you met . . . ?" Then he hesitated, turned to me, and asked, "How do I introduce you? Are you 'Doctor,' 'Dean,' 'Professor,' or what?"

"How about Mister?" I responded.

To which he replied, in a scathing tone, "Nobody is just 'Mister'!"

On our last vacation we returned to our hotel in Chicago late one night to discover that my daughter's key would not open her door. Various telephone calls downstairs produced vague promises that the maintenance man would be sought and sent to our rescue. Various vague accusations of incompetence were also made—were we sure we had the right key? Were we sure we had the right door? Finally, an irate father, I descended to the lobby to demand more concrete assistance. Imagine my astonishment when I was advised by a sober room clerk that the real cause of our problem was the refusal of a credit card company to honor my charge. "But," I expostulated, "I didn't use that credit card when I checked in." He looked at me pityingly and waved a form at me, pointing to the corner where, indeed, my daughter's room number was inscribed. Then my eye caught the name on the form; it was not Schoonover! "That's not my name," I shouted, again to disbelieving looks from the clerk. After all, the "right" number was on the form; what difference did it make if the name was "wrong"? (The number, too, of course was "wrong"; the poor credit risk apparently was sleeping soundly three floors above!)

Who am I? So much of the time we are left to sing a lament about "The Me Nobody Knows," unknown, essentially, even to ourselves.

Even in the church we are guilty of playing that game. For the past eight years my ministry has been one to battered, bleeding, and bewildered clergy. They have so thoroughly internalized the rhetoric of the church—"you are a sinner"—that they know down deep in their bones that the overwhelming reality is that they are "no damn good."

When that understanding of human life gets acted out openly, as in the latest musical and social phenomenon in England called "punk rock," it is little short of terrifying. Here are young people declaring in their music and in their behavior that there are no human values; indeed, there is nothing of value. Chic clothing is considered to be rags, sometimes deliberately created by expensive boutiques, and the proper human relationship—whether in dancing or love-making—is to abuse physically the other person. That, I would contend, is only a caricature—an exaggeration—of much of our society.

Who am I?

I wonder how Peter saw himself? I wonder if he ever thought of himself as "only a crude fisherman" or "only an impetuous person who speaks before he thinks" or "only a betrayer of the Son of God"? He was all of those things. Yet he was a lot more, and Jesus could see deep into Peter's soul and know that beneath everything else was a rock of potentiality on which it was even possible to build the church of God. In learning from Jesus, Peter finally came to believe in this power and to walk steadfastly where the Lord would have him go, even ultimately to his own cruel death.

Our identities are in a real sense conferred upon us. It is terribly important, then, who does the conferring. As his "body" in the world, in ways the church hardly recognizes, it "binds" and "looses" people in the manner in which it affirms both their identities and that of Jesus.

I am persuaded that the way for human beings to discover who they really are is first to discover who Jesus is. So the dialogue between Jesus and us continues. *Who do people say I am?* What answers might we give? *Some say you are a nice, gentle man who loves everybody and never gets angry. Others say you are a revolutionary model who can lead people out of bondage to all kinds of political, social, and economic systems.* I am sure all of us can supply more variations.

Insistently—because it really matters what the answer is—Jesus presses the next question, "Who do you say I am?" If our response can come to be that he is Christ—the Messiah of God—then, in his service, we shall be able to learn who we are, learn to think as God thinks, learn to see as God sees, learn to act as he acts so that in both heaven and earth what he wills may be done. One day we shall know without doubt that any identity which is modified by the word "only" is wrong.

Who am I? Who are you? We have some notions already of what other people say. What do you suppose Jesus will say?

The question I want to pose in relation to this biblical passage is, "What if who we are depends on who Jesus is?"

When Jesus came to Caesarea Philippi, he asked his disciples, "Who do people say that the Son of Man is?"

They answered, "Some say you are John the Baptist. Others say you are Elijah, and still others say you are Jeremiah come back to life or one of the other prophets."

"And you," he asked, "who do you say I am?"

Simon Peter answered, "You are the Messiah, the Christ, the Son of the living God."

Then Jesus said, "Simon, son of John, you have been richly blessed. Flesh and blood—human understanding—is not the source of this knowledge. My heavenly father has revealed this to you. And I say this to you: You are Peter, the Rock, and on this rock I will build my church—and all the powers of evil and death shall never prevail against it. I will give to you the keys of the kingdom of Heaven; and what you forbid on earth will be forbidden in heaven, and what you permit on earth shall be allowed in heaven."

Then he gave his disciples strict orders not to tell anyone that he was the Messiah.

From that time on, Jesus began to make it clear to his disciples that he had to go to Jerusalem and there would suffer greatly at the hands of the religious authorities, be put to death, and on the third day be raised to new life. Peter grabbed his arm and began to rebuke him for saying such things. "No, Lord, these things will not happen to you."

Then Jesus turned and said to Peter, "Get away from me, Satan; you are a stumbling block to me. You think as men think, not as God thinks."

2

Capernaum:

Human Hungers

New York mayoral primary elections are almost always colorful, and the last one was no exception. There was a plethora of candidates for what most rational people feel is an administratively impossible and politically dead-end job. Among the hopefuls were the same incompetent bookkeeper who brought us to the verge of bankruptcy, a woman noted equally for her large hats and her large mouth, a cigar-store-type wooden Hispanic, a decent public-servant type whose name to the end produced a look of ignorance on most voters' faces, and a smooth-talking black politician whose chief claim to fame was that he had managed to get himself reelected to office no matter who was at the top of his party's ticket. Oh, yes, there was also the heir to the Ex-Lax fortune. Imagine choosing your mayor for the next four years from that list! Actually we did not; the successful candidate was a quite colorless congressman whose candidacy few people took seriously until he managed to sweep the primary, the runoff, and the general election.

I mention them only to say that to election day they struggled to find "the issue" to capture the imagination of the voters. Oh, they tried. The incumbent bookkeeper ran against "the bosses," especially those associated with the governor who sought to replace those associated with the mayor. The wooden Hispanic (who also happens to be a bookkeeper) ran against the incompetent bookkeeper. The decent public servant ran on the side of "good government." The Ex-Lax heir promised to "clean up the city." The smooth-talking black ran against crime in the streets.

The last one, at least, struck some response with people, for people were tired of being victimized by crime wherever it happens. One had to admire his courage in insisting after the blackout looting that the issue the city had to deal with was criminal and not racial. All this did not, however, keep people from asking what he had been doing through all the years he had been in public office, years in which the crime rate had soared.

Oddly enough, the successful candidate won the primary because of his ringing endorsement of capital punishment. The voters, apparently, wanted their government to get *really* tough with criminals. It seemed to impress no one that the mayor of New York is powerless to institute such draconian policy.

The people of New York express the same longings, mirror the same hungers as every human group. They are like the people of first-century Palestine who flocked around Jesus for help and we turn now to learn again of the hungers they brought to him to be satisfied.

This time we are in Capernaum, an important town on the northern shore of the Sea of Galilee. Nothing is known about the town except what is told us in the Gospels. It was obviously an important trading center, for there was a customs station; and it is assumed that Matthew, one of the original disciples, worked here as a tax collector. It was also an important center for fishing; on nearby beaches Jesus had recruited Simon Peter and Andrew to follow him.

There was a body of Roman soldiers stationed in the town. The commander, Luke tells us, ingratiated himself with the people there by building them a synagogue. "An officer of the royal service" lived there and Jesus' healing of his son was one of the early miracles recorded in John.

Indeed, the town is primarily known because of its association with Jesus. After John the Baptist's execution, Jesus appears to have settled in Capernaum. Matthew interprets this as a calculated action designed to fulfill the prediction of Isaiah that the new Light of Israel would come from Galilee. After his rejection in Nazareth, Jesus made Capernaum his permanent headquarters—Matthew refers to it subsequently as "his own city" and Mark speaks of Jesus as being "at home" when he was there.

Capernaum clearly played an important role in the development of Jesus' ministry. Not only did it provide several, if not most, of his inner group of disciples, but Capernaum was also the setting for many miracles, including the healing of Simon Peter's mother-in-law and the casting out the "unclean spirit" of the man in the synagogue. Here also Jesus taught his disciples a great lesson in humility by bringing a child into their midst, around whom he put his arm, saying, "Whoever receives me, receives not me but the One who sent me."

In and around Capernaum, John's Gospel sets a series of episodes dealing with things for which people hunger. To these we now turn.

Some time later Jesus withdrew to the farther shore of the Sea of Galilee (or Tiberias), and a large crowd of people followed who had seen the signs he performed in healing the sick. Then Jesus went up the hillside and sat down with his disciples. It was near the time of Passover, the great Jewish festival. Raising his eyes and seeing a large crowd coming towards him, Jesus said to Philip, "Where are we to buy bread to feed these people?" This he said to test him; Jesus himself knew what he meant to do. Philip replied, "Two hundred denarii would not buy enough bread for every one of them to have a little." One of his disciples, Andrew, the brother of Simon Peter, said to him, "There is a boy here who has five barley loaves and two fishes; but what is that among so many?" Jesus said, "Make the people sit down." There was plenty of grass there, so the men sat down, about five thousand of them. Then Jesus took the loaves, gave thanks, and distributed them to the people as they sat there. He did the same with the fishes, and they had as much as they wanted. When everyone had had enough, he said to his disciples, "Collect the pieces left over, so that nothing may be lost." This they did, and filled twelve baskets with the pieces left uneaten of the five barley loaves.

When the people saw the sign Jesus had performed, the word went round, "Surely this must be the prophet that was to come into the world." Jesus, aware that they meant to come and seize him to proclaim him king, withdrew again to the hills by himself.

At nightfall his disciples went down to the sea, got into their boat, and pushed off to cross the water to Capernaum. Darkness had already fallen, and Jesus had not yet joined them. By now a strong wind was blowing and the sea grew rough. When they had rowed about three or four miles they saw Jesus walking on the sea and approaching the boat. They were terrified, but he called out, "It is I; do not be afraid." Then they were ready to take him aboard, and immediately the boat reached the land they were making for.

Next morning the crowd was standing on the opposite shore. They had seen only one boat there, and Jesus, they knew, had not embarked with his disciples, who had gone away without him. Boats from Tiberias, however, came ashore near the place where the people had eaten the bread over which the Lord gave thanks. When the people saw that neither Jesus nor his disciples were any longer there, they themselves went aboard these boats and made for Capernaum in search of Jesus. They found him on the other side. "Rabbi," they said, "when did you come here?" Jesus replied, "In very truth I know that you have not come looking for me because you saw signs, but because you ate the bread and your hunger was satisfied. You must work, not for this perishable food, but for the food that lasts, the food of eternal life.

"This food the Son of Man will give you, for he it is upon whom God the Father has set the seal of his authority." "Then what must we do," they asked him, "if we are to work as God would have us work?" Jesus replied, "This is the work that God requires: believe in the one whom he has sent."

They said, "What sign can you give us to see, so that we may believe you? What is the work you do? Our ancestors had manna to eat in the desert; as Scripture says, 'He gave them bread from heaven to eat.'" Jesus answered, "I tell you this; the truth is, not that Moses gave you the bread from heaven, but that my Father gives you the real bread from heaven. The bread that God gives comes down from heaven and brings life to the world." They said to him, "Sir, give us this bread now and always." Jesus said to them, "I am the bread of life. Whoever comes to me shall never be hungry, and whoever believes in me shall never be thirsty. But you, as I said, do not believe although you have seen. All that the Father gives me will come to me, and the man who comes to me I will never turn away. I have come down from heaven, not to do my own will, but the will of him who sent me. It is his will that I should not lose even one of all that he has given me, but raise them all up on the last day. For it is my Father's will that everyone who looks upon the Son and puts his faith in him shall possess eternal life; and I will raise him up on the last day."

At this the Jews began to murmur disapprovingly because he said, "I am the bread which came down from heaven." They said, "Surely this is Jesus son of Joseph; we know his father and mother. How can he now say, 'I have come down from heaven'?" Jesus answered, "Stop murmuring among yourselves. No man can come to me unless he is drawn by the Father who sent me; and I will raise him up on the last day. It is written in the prophets: 'And they shall all be taught by God.' Everyone who has listened to the Father and learned from him comes to me.

"I do not mean that anyone has seen the Father. He who has come from God has seen the Father, and he alone. In truth, in very truth I tell you, the believer possesses eternal life. I am the bread of life. Your forefathers ate the manna in the desert and they are dead. I am speaking of the bread that comes down from heaven, which a man may eat, and never die. I am that living bread which has come down from heaven; if anyone eats this bread he shall live for ever. Moreover, the bread which I will give is my own flesh; I give it for the life of the world."

This led to a fierce dispute among the Jews. "How can this man give us his flesh to eat?" they said. Jesus replied, "In truth, in very truth I tell you, unless you eat the flesh of the Son of Man and drink his blood you can have no life in you. Whoever eats my flesh and drinks my blood possesses eternal life, and I will raise him up on the last day. My flesh is real food; my blood is real drink. Whoever eats my flesh and drinks my blood dwells continually in me and I dwell in him. As the living Father sent me, and I live because of the Father, so he who eats me shall live because of me. This is the bread which came down from heaven; and it is not like the bread which our fathers ate: they are dead, but whoever eats this bread shall live for ever."

This was spoken in synagogue when Jesus was teaching in Capernaum. Many of his disciples on hearing it exclaimed, "This is more than we can stomach! Why listen to such talk?" Jesus was aware that his disciples were murmuring about it and asked them, "Does this shock you? What if you see the Son of Man ascending to the place where he was before? The spirit alone gives life; the flesh is of no avail; the words which I have spoken to you are both spirit and life. And yet there are some of you who have no faith." For Jesus knew all along who were without faith and who was to betray him. So he said, "This is why I told you that no one can come to me unless it has been granted to him by the Father."

From that time on, many of his disciples withdrew and no longer went about with him. So Jesus asked the Twelve, "Do you also want to leave me?" Simon Peter answered him, "Lord, to whom shall we go? Your words are words of eternal life. We have faith, and we know that you are the Holy One of God." Jesus answered, "Have I not chosen you, all twelve? Yet one of you is a devil." He meant Judas, son of Simon Iscariot. He it was who would betray him, and he was one of the Twelve (John 6).

Jesus and his disciples have withdrawn to a deserted place on the other side of the lake. Matthew attributes their going to the need to mourn John the Baptist, of whose murder word has just come. Luke and Mark, however, associate it with the return of the apostles from their missionary labors, after which (according to Mark) Jesus desires them to have a time of rest. Doubtless, too, there is the need for an uninterrupted period of "debriefing"; and experience is already abundant that, if people know where Jesus is, he will be subject to constant interruptions.

Even now a large crowd follows. Are they the ordinary curious? Are they pilgrims on the way to Jerusalem for the Passover festivities? The scholars disagree; Raymond Brown is dubious that they were pilgrims because Capernaum was not on any pilgrim route people would take to the capital. Furthermore, he says, pilgrims would have been carrying food.[7]

Sitting on the hillside and watching the throngs of people approaching, Jesus inquires of Philip how they are to feed so many. Someone has speculated that literal-minded Philip calculated the money the disciples had among them and decided even if they spent it all on bread in one of the nearby villages it would not be enough. He would just be the first of thousands of trustees who decided that the church was too poor to meet the needs of the people pressing in all around!

Andrew, another of the disciples, announces that a boy who perhaps has overheard this conversation has offered his lunch—five small barley loaves (the cheap, coarse food of the poor) and a couple of pickled fish. Since he, too, is a "practical" man, one can imagine that he is amused by the idealistic generosity of the child.

Jesus, too, is practical but not amused. He quickly organizes the chaotic crowd by getting the people to sit down in groups on the grass. There were probably more than five thousand men, women, and children for it is said that there were five thousand men. Then Jesus takes the boy's lunch, blesses the bread and the fish, and begins to pass them among the people. However it happens—miraculous multiplication of the food on the one hand (which John probably intends to convey) or a spontaneous sharing of other lunches among the crowd on the other—apparently there is total amazement at the end because, miraculously, everyone is fed and there is food left over.

There is no great amount, to be sure. The "baskets" referred to are only the small traveling cases individuals would carry on a journey, big enough for the day's food. Curiously enough, there are twelve basketfuls—enough for the disciples. Evelyn Underhill commented, "No waste, but no stinginess. God does not starve His staff; He always leaves them, if they follow His plan for them and give without reserve to His children, with enough food in hand for the day. Give without reserve, and you will gather up enough to fill your own lunch basket!"[8]

The crowd is impressed with what happens. Like wildfire the word spreads that Jesus must be the Messiah. Their bellies full and their hopes for deliverance from oppression quickened, people begin to talk about forcing him to become their king. Their desperation, their eagerness is great. Josephus told of two total charlatans: Theudas, who said he could cause the waters of the Jordan to part, and an Egyptian who said he could cause the walls of Jerusalem to collapse so that the city would fall. Both were frauds, easily dispatched by Roman forces. Yet people eagerly followed both; their yearning for release from captivity was so great they would seize on any promise or sign. So, completely misunderstanding the significance of the feeding of the five thousand, the people are determined Jesus is to be their king. Is not this a sign of the era of earthly abundance which the prophets had foretold? "We batter at the door of heaven," William Temple wrote, "demanding audience for our proposals whereby God may save His World, or promote His purpose. But faith consists in leaving Him to take His own way."[9] So Jesus slips away to the hills to be alone.

Meanwhile the disciples have also departed. Under cover of darkness, they have gone down to the shore and pushed off in a boat toward Capernaum. As often happens, a sudden squall blows up and the water becomes rough. They struggle to keep the boat afloat and head toward their destination. So great is their preoccupation that they do not see Jesus until he calls out reassuringly. Then they see they have reached their destination.

It is interesting to observe here that John, who never hesitates to claim supernatural powers for Jesus, does not necessarily picture this episode as being unique. The Greek can mean that Jesus walked "by the sea"; we could assume that he has walked around the northern portion of the Sea of Galilee, moving along faster than the disciples have been able to row in the storm. Some scholars say that there is no way of explaining their "terror" unless, as Matthew and Mark picture it, Jesus is seen defying natural forces and walking on the water itself. Yet others—like A. M. Hunter[10]—explain it as quite a natural phenomenon. Believe what you wish or must; in either case, remember that the importance of this section of the chapter is that, when the disciples come to the end of their journey, Jesus is there to meet them.

The next morning, finding that neither Jesus nor his disciples are with them, some of the people get into newly arrived boats and set off to Capernaum to try to find him. When they find him there, they begin to question him about how he had gotten there. Jesus declines to satisfy their curiosity and launches into an attack on their motives for seeking him out. They have come, he says, for another free meal. *You must not settle for that,* he says, *instead of food which will still leave you hungry in a while, work for the food of eternal life. That's the food I will give you, for God the Father has put his everlasting seal of approval on what I do.*

What shall we do, the people ask, *in order to do the work God expects of us?*

The answer is brief, simple, demanding, pointed—the same now, as then—*Believe in me.*

I confess I have some sympathy for the crowd in what happens next. They have been burned before. Loren Mead described to our faculty recently the "seduction/disappointment" cycle that every church goes through with every new pastor. There is a mutual seduction process that goes on in which everything is promised, everything expected. Then the honeymoon ends, and there is mutual disappointment. Things are not quite like people expected; things have not quite worked out as promised. Disillusionment results. These people have been disappointed before; they are wary. So they ask for more signs that he is indeed the Messiah. Moses who was not the Messiah had been able to produce manna in the desert day by day. The implication is that surely Jesus can do as well in multiplying the signs of his authority.

Jesus is outraged. I can understand that, too. The Son of God cannot be expected to perform like a magician. He is not at our beck and call. Instead he beckons to us and calls us to trust him and follow him on the basis of what he has already shown us and of what we know and hope. There can be no conditions to our discipleship.

It was not Moses who gave your ancestors manna in the desert, Jesus says, *it came from God. God is still giving life-providing bread from heaven.*

"Give it to us, sir," the people plead, "give it to us now and always."

"I am the bread of life," Jesus responds. "Whoever comes to me shall never be hungry, and whoever believes in me shall never be thirsty." Then Jesus observes, sadly, *You don't believe, do you? Those whom my father has given me will indeed come to me, and anyone who comes to me I will never turn away. I have come to do my father's will, and it is my father's will that I should not lose even one person. My father wills that everyone who has faith in me shall possess eternal life. To them I will guarantee resurrection on the day of judgment.*

At this point, we are told, there began to be "murmurings" of disapproval. Several things played a role, no doubt. His promise of the gift of resurrection alone would have offended many of his hearers. It was a cardinal tenet of the "fundamental" faith among the Sadducees, for instance, that there would be no resurrection of the dead. They were, if you will pardon the intentional pun, willing to stake their lives on it. These were people who were convinced they knew precisely what God was about and what he demanded of his people, and they were absolutely certain Jesus did not fit in that picture. Indeed, he was a very dangerous figure who, if left alone, would destroy Judaism as they knew, loved, and prospered from it. Their formulations of the faith were so rehearsed that Jesus had only to mention one of their sacred code words, and they would be off on a mindless tirade of resistance. Their descendants are among us.

Others resisted Jesus because he did not fit their preconceptions of what the Messiah would be like. Increasingly the issue of the warrior king came to the fore in his ministry. The witness of prophets like Isaiah and Zechariah was far less familiar and acceptable than that of Jeremiah and Elijah. People wanted familiar tradition in their religion, but militancy and action in their politics. Jesus' claims about himself appear to them to be so arrogant. *I am the bread come down from heaven,* he says.

To which their response is, *You've got to be kidding. We know who you are—we know your parents, Mary and Joseph.* Is that not all we need to know to label any person definitively and finally? *We know all we need to know about you, Jesus—you are Mary's and Joseph's son.* The impossibility of extraordinary things happening in ordinary circumstances and relationships weighs heavily on literal-minded folk. How can he now say, "I have come down from heaven"? Their descendants are among us, also.

The outcry against him causes Jesus to say, in effect, *Shut up! Listen, for your lives and destinies depend on it! If what I say makes any sense, it is because of what God is saying through me. Everyone who has listened to the Father and learned from him comes to me.* Then Jesus heightens the mystery and the conflict further by saying that only *he* has seen the Father. Eternal life is assured for those who fully accept the one sent from God. *I am the bread of life. Our forefathers ate the manna in the wilderness, but now they are dead. Do you not understand? They are dead! God is now providing a "living bread" which will provide eternal life for those who believe. I am that living bread which has come down from heaven; if anyone eats this bread he shall live forever.* This "bread," Jesus says, is his own flesh. Here, then, we have John's version of words so dramatic a hush comes in our churches whenever we repeat them: "This is my body, broken for you."

That, in turn, reminds us of another statement from Scripture which people approach thoughtfully and wonderingly: "In the beginning was the Word. . . . The Word became flesh and dwelt among us, full of grace and truth; we have beheld his glory, glory as of the only Son from the Father" (John 1:1, 14, RSV).

God's life, then, is offered for incorporation into our lives through the incarnation. The term "flesh" stands for the fullness of humanity—its totality, leaving nothing out. It is by his humanity that Jesus offers us life; if we receive it and it fully becomes our own, it is found to bring with it the gift of eternal life. "The bread which I give is my own flesh. I give it for the life of the world."

Eternal life, Jesus seems to be saying, is the possession only of those who have passed beyond reliance upon the physical senses into the experience of spiritual perception, namely faith. Life in that dimension is only sustained by spiritual food, unlike the manna which lasted for a day and then was spoiled. The living bread which Jesus represents endures and sustains. It is the life of Jesus, given up freely, which springs up whenever people believe in him in the world and which, ultimately, will become the life of the world itself.

When people are in love and fellowship with one another, they can speak in metaphorical terms and be understood. When people hate one another and are hostile, they resort to legalistic literalism. So "the Jews"—a code word in John for that group of leaders who opposed Jesus to the death—accuse Jesus of advocating some kind of crude cannibalism. To eat someone's flesh is a metaphor both in the Psalms and in the prophet Zechariah for hostile action, and there was an Aramaic tradition which called the Devil an "eater of flesh." Since "the Jews" detest Jesus and consider him a danger to everything they believe, they resort to violent outcries of opposition.

Jesus apparently decides to make an issue of this concept of "heavenly food" personified in himself and, indeed, further escalates the argument to a level which almost seems designed to drive his opponents into frenzy. "In truth . . . unless you eat the flesh of the Son of Man and drink his blood you can have no life in you. Whoever eats my flesh and drinks my blood. . . . My flesh is real food; my blood is real drink. Whoever eats my flesh and drinks my blood. . . ." Over and over again he pounds away at a metaphor that he knows; because of their unyielding theological position, they cannot accept. If to eat his flesh was cannibalism to the literal-minded, to drink his blood would cause them to violate an explicit law of God handed down through the centuries—a total, unambiguous ban on the consumption of blood. It is hard for most of us to understand the intensity of feeling about this. We encounter it tangentially through the occasional Orthodox Jew we might meet or through reading of still another court decision ordering life-giving blood transfusions for the child of a Jehovah's Witness. For Jesus' hearers, the ban on eating blood was the most powerful taboo in the world, for blood was the bearer of life.

Can't you make it easier for people, Jesus? Do you have to make the choice so extreme, so decisive, so clear? People really do like ambiguity, for then they can read their own meaning into the situation. But you make it hard for us. You require a clear choice. What was that you said? *Blessed are those who are not offended by me.*

Well, many were offended by Jesus that day. "This is more than we can stomach"—*this teaching is hard, harsh, fantastic, offensive. Why listen to such talk?* There in the synagogue in Capernaum, surrounded by the symbols of Israel's longtime love affair with Yahweh, even many of Jesus' disciples were offended by him and left him. Yes, the very same ones who had come with him to detail their experiences of victory and defeat as his missionaries in the world. *Does this shock you—does this shake your faith?*—is the rhetorical question Jesus asks, for he already knows the answer. They are so shocked they can think of only one thing, and that is to get far, far away from this madman. *What if* . . . Jesus begins anew. *What if what I have said to you about the relationship I have with my Father happens to be true? Only the Spirit can reveal that to you, the Spirit who alone provides the real substance to flesh and blood. I have spoken of "spiritual things" to you; yet some of you have no faith. You see, I was right before when I said no one comes to me unless it is at the Father's initiative.*

So there he is, alone with the twelve, "Do you also want to leave me?"

Again it is Peter who serves as spokesman (this is John's equivalent to the episode we considered in the first chapter). "Lord, to whom shall we go?" *Who else could possibly compete with you for our loyalty?* "Your words are words of eternal life." *Only your words have kindled our faith and given us a vision of the eternal kingdom.* "We"—the Greek is emphatic—" have faith, and we know that you are the Holy One of God." *You are not just the long-expected Messiah; you personify the spiritual character of God himself.*

These are ironic words, in retrospect. Soon *all* of the disciples would leave Jesus. Peter, who would soon be called "Satan" by his Lord, would soon deny him. "How near," as William Temple said, "the saint is to the sinner!"[11] Judas, who remains as an enemy within the ranks of this group of friends, would betray him. Now Jesus engages in a bit of bittersweet reflection. *I chose you all. . . . One of you is a devil. . . .* The chapter ends with these painful words: "He meant Judas, son of Simon Iscariot. He it was who would betray him, and he was one of the Twelve."

When one lives in New York, one gets the feeling one is surrounded by devils—malevolent people and forces who seek the destruction of the city and everything for which it stands. At times it seems that no one cares about our fate; no one feels one whit of concern or compassion for our problems; no one gives a thought to our dreams and aspirations. We hunger for many things, but there is no food.

Abraham Maslow, the great motivational psychologist, has proposed that humankind, in the course of a lifetime, exhibits six basic needs. The first is *physiological*—we must have food and drink in order to survive. Next to that most basic need is the need for *safety*—we need security, order, and stability in life in order to function. Then, Maslow says, the need for *love and belonging* follows—we need warmth, affection, the knowledge that some other people care for and about us and are willing to include us in their "family." Maslow's fourth basic human need is *identity*—we need self-respect, self-esteem, some successes. Then there is the need for *commitment*—we need some focus, some direction in our lives. Finally, he says, there is the need for *self-actualization*—we need to feel creative and independent, that what we do makes a difference and that somehow we can shape that doing, if not totally control it.

Maslow says that these needs emerge in the "normal life" at somewhat clearly defined, chronological periods. They are sequential, each, in a sense, growing out of and being a more highly sophisticated expression of what has gone before. Since life is very dynamic and we have our "ups and downs," we flit back and forth among the levels we have attained—sometimes needing satisfaction of more fundamental and basic needs, sometimes feeling secure enough to explore the more highly differentiated needs. The emotionally healthy person, however, is throughout his or her life moving from the satisfaction of physiological needs toward satisfaction of the needs of self-actualization. The church can profit greatly from taking Maslow's insights seriously.

For the fun of it, I reread John 6 in the light of Maslow's categories. It seems to me that they are all there. Abundant emphasis is placed on the need for food. In the course of that long conversation, however, the needs of first-century Jews for survival, healing, and both national and economic security are dealt with in some detail; then the need for acceptance and community; then the need for making sense of life and one's relationship to it; then the need for a concept of eternal life; then the need for control of nature and the need for freedom. This rich chapter portrays a very complex set of personal and corporate needs. To all these Jesus says, *Come, I am the bread of life.*

New Yorkers, like people in many other cities, are tired and have many needs. They long for relief from grinding poverty that afflicts approximately one out of six persons. They long for a reversal in the gushing flow of jobs *from* the city. They are hungry for personal safety on the streets, in the subways, in their homes.

They hunger for people to say a good word about them, instead of always making them the butt of a joke or the objects of hostility. They long for people to understand that their fiscal problems are caused as much by the willingness of other parts of the country to export their unwanted "problems" as it is by New York's "pampering" of the undeserving poor. They long for people to recognize that because of the tax structures they still subsidize others elsewhere who attack them most.

They yearn for cessation of those forces that seem beyond their control, which result in progressive deterioration of the quality of city life. They long for new "handles" on how to absorb the latest wave of those seeking after personal and political freedom. They seek for ways of preserving the existing middle class, remaining in the city, as well as ways of creating a new one from the masses of poor.

They yearn for healing of their infirmities, companionship for their old age, cessation of oppressive dehumanization and resulting loneliness. They yearn for a little peace and quiet, a little self-respect, a little relief from whatever oppresses them, a little hope for tomorrow.

To all these human hungers, I am convinced that Jesus is still saying, *Come, I am the bread of life.*

Jesus brings this message, but the church frequently does not. The church seems often in the position of saying that *none* of these hungers is important. Only the hunger for personal salvation is important. One of the consequences, I believe, is that our churches are sparsely populated and membership seems to have little meaning to many people.

Commenting on the church in Europe (which is further along in decay than ours), Carl Jung once wrote, "A clever European is convinced that religion and such things are good enough for the masses and for women, but are of little weight compared to economic and political affairs."[12]

To limit Christ's concern to "spiritual things," in any narrow interpretation of that phrase, is just unreal. For those who, wrapped in their own pure religion (clean but unhelpful), pass by on the other side of human crisis, his scorn can never be forgotten or minimized. Nor can we forget the sharp questions which Jesus assures us will be put to us at the judgment seat, questions not about prayer and doctrine and "spiritual" things at all, but about the practical help and unselfishness which must flow from us if his spirit is our spirit.

So let me share a couple of personal hungers. I hunger for a climate in the church which does not polarize people on the basis of personal evangelism versus social action but that affirms with conviction and power that there is one gospel just as there is one God and one Lord—and that what really decides whether either evangelism or social action is Christian is the spirit which infuses and informs all our actions and beliefs.

I hunger also for a church so dedicated to the Lord that it will be concerned about everything that affects the welfare of God's people. I hunger for a church that will not just "shoot from the hip" like a church leader in New York does in his Easter sermons, denouncing those wicked businesses that leave our city, but a church which helps in whatever way it can those followers of the Christ who sit in high places to seek the will of the Lord. I hunger for the church to "do theology" about what is happening in this world—to help people to understand and to plan and to hope for the implementation of the kingdom and, at the end, to help us with our experiences of betrayal and death.

I hunger for a community that can give itself for the world because it has given itself to Jesus Christ, the one who has given himself for the world. The Japanese saint of the last generation, Kagawa, asked the question once: "What are you doing with *your* body and blood? That's all God has."

Jesus said, *Come, I am the bread of life. I give it for the life of the world. . . .*

So the question this episode poses is: "What if Jesus is really Lord of *every* aspect of our lives?"

Jesus and his disciples had withdrawn for some rest but were pursued by great throngs of people. Despite the apparent lack of resources, everyone was fed as much as he or she needed, with enough left over to provide food for the disciples. So impressed were the people that some acclaimed Jesus as the long-expected deliverer of Israel and sought to force him to become their king, but Jesus slipped away from them.

After a hard night of rowing in a storm on the Sea of Galilee, the disciples were terrified when Jesus suddenly appeared to them in the darkness; but he calmed their fears with a few words.

The next morning some of the people who had been fed the evening before followed Jesus to Capernaum. Jesus rebuked them for seeking him out only to get another free meal. Instead, he said, they should seek for eternal food which would never leave them hungry. "Give us this food," the people responded; and Jesus said, "I am the bread of life. Whoever comes to me shall never be hungry. Whoever believes in me shall never be thirsty."

People were perplexed, saying, "Is this not Joseph's son?" People were bewildered, asking, "Is he advocating cannibalism?" People were scandalized, saying, "How can he defy our law and speak of drinking his blood?"

This dialogue took place in the synagogue in Capernaum. Even many of his disciples said, "This is more than we can stomach! Why listen to such talk?"

Jesus was aware of their unrest and asked them, "Does this shock you? What if you see the Son of Man ascending to the place where he was before? The spirit alone gives life; the flesh alone is of no avail; my words are both spirit and life. And yet there are some of you who have no faith."

For Jesus knew all along who were without faith and who would betray him. So he said, "This is why I have told you that no one can come to me unless it has been granted to him by the Father."

From that time on, many of his disciples withdrew from the movement and no longer went about with him.

So Jesus asked the Twelve, "Do you also want to leave me?"

Simon Peter answered him, "Lord, to whom shall we go? Your words alone are words of eternal life. We have faith, and we know that you are the Holy One of God."

Jesus replied, "Have I not chosen you all, all Twelve? Yet one of you is a devil." He meant Judas, son of Simon Iscariot. He it was who would betray him, and he was one of the Twelve.

—

3

Nazareth and Tyre:

Who Belongs?

Recently I met with a group of Bates College students who were winding up a six-week study and work project in East Harlem. Among them was a tiny, pert young woman—the kind of person you would instantly guess would add good humor and liveliness to any group. She appeared to be troubled on this occasion. Finally she shared what was bothering her.

On the day before, at her job site, she had found herself in unexpected and unintentional conflict with a black woman. The details are unimportant. What is important is what was said and the effect of the words. The black woman said to the Bates student: "Why don't you go back to Maine or Spain or wherever you belong?"

The young white student was devastated, and her question to me was: "Where do I belong?"

"Where do I belong?" That is another question with which the people of faith have wrestled for centuries. Our spiritual and biological ancestors have fought many a bloody battle to secure particular bits of geography in the conviction that God has said, "This is where you belong," Further bloody battles have then been fought to defend that "promised land" against others who protested that they had the same message from the Lord. So the question is also *who* belongs?

That is the issue in Jesus' urban ministry which we consider in this chapter. Two cities are involved, for this episode in Jesus' ministry has two necessary parts.

One is Nazareth. It apparently was, as now, a backwater kind of place that no one would seek out while on a trip. It was not on any main traffic route. Indeed, again, our knowledge of it comes only through its connection with the life of Jesus.

Both Mary and Joseph lived in Nazareth, and it was here that Luke says the angel Gabriel appeared to Mary to announce Jesus' birth. Joseph traveled from Nazareth to Bethlehem when Caesar decided to make the unproductive citizens of Palestine go to their ancestral homes to be counted for the purpose of efficient taxation. The family returned to Nazareth after its side journey to Egypt, according to Matthew, to satisfy the prophecy that the Christ should come from among the Nazarenes. From Nazareth Jesus went to be baptized in the Jordan by John, and to Nazareth he returned following his period of temptation in the wilderness. That is all we really know about the town.

Tyre, on the other hand, was quite different. It was an ancient seaport (the earliest *written* records date back 3,500 years!), a Gentile community which had prospered through the centuries from carrying "the trade of nations to many coasts and islands" (as Ezekiel put it) and "whose merchants were princes and her traders the most honoured men on earth" (in the words of Isaiah). It had been a pawn in the struggles for domination of the Middle East between the Egyptians and the Syrians, and it is described in many places in the Old Testament as being heavily fortified and strong. Nebuchadnezzar II besieged it for three years before Tyre acknowledged domination by Babylon. Even Alexander the Great required seven months to beat down Tyre's resistance to invasion.

Its chief fame was commercial, however, not political or military. The city was long famous for its glass, its dyes, and its shipbuilding. King Hiram was friendly with both David and Solomon and provided materials for the building of Jerusalem. Another Hiram, of mixed Tyranian and Hebrew parentage, cast pillars for the temple.

Jezebel, wife of Ahab, was daughter of still another king of Tyre and introduced the worship of Baal to Israel.

The Romans assumed power over Tyre in 68 B.C., but it was still a rich, powerful, and populous city in Jesus' day. One sign of its tolerant spirit was that early in Jesus' ministry men of Tyre went out to Galilee to hear him. Indeed, Jesus declared that if its people had been favored like the cities of Galilee, they would have flocked to repentance and discipleship.

Now let us consider the first of the two related episodes.

So he came to Nazareth, where he had been brought up, and went to synagogue on the Sabbath day as he regularly did. He stood up to read the lesson and was handed the scroll of the prophet Isaiah. He opened the scroll and found the passage which says,

"The spirit of the Lord is upon me
　because he has anointed me;
he has sent me to announce good news to the poor,
to proclaim release for prisoners and recovery of
　sight for the blind;
to let the broken victims go free,
to proclaim the year of the Lord's favour."

He rolled up the scroll, gave it back to the attendant, and sat down; and all eyes in the synagogue were fixed on him.

He began to speak: "Today," he said, "in your very hearing this text has come true." There was a general stir of admiration; they were surprised that words of such grace should fall from his lips. "Is not this Joseph's son?" they asked. Then Jesus said, "No doubt you will quote the proverb to me, 'Physician, heal yourself!', and say, 'We have heard of all your doings at Capernaum; do the same here in your own home town.' I tell you this," he went on: "no prophet is recognized in his own country. There were many widows in Israel, you may be sure, in Elijah's time, when for three years and six months the skies never opened, and famine lay hard over the whole country; yet it was to none of those that Elijah was sent, but to a widow at Sarepta in the territory of Sidon. Again, in the time of the prophet Elisha there were many lepers in Israel, and not one of them was healed, but only Naaman, the Syrian." At these words the whole congregation were infuriated. They leapt up, threw him out of the town, and took him to the brow of the hill on which it was built, meaning to hurl him over the edge. But he walked straight through them all, and went away (Luke 4:16-30).

The first part of our two-part "event" is recorded in Luke's Gospel and concerns the appearance of Jesus in the synagogue in Nazareth. As is his practice, we are told, he goes to the sabbath service. (It is interesting to note that Luke uses the same introductory phrase— "as was his custom"—once more in referring to Jesus' going to the Garden of Gethsemane to pray.)

Worship in the synagogue began with the recitation of the Shema ("Hear, O Israel, the Lord is our God, one Lord, and you must love the Lord your God with all your heart and soul and strength" [Deuteronomy 6:4-5]—which Jesus said was the first and greatest commandment). Then there would be a prayer followed by a prescribed reading from the Law—something from the Pentateuch, the first five books of the Old Testament. It is presumed that the readings from the Law were set up in such a way as to cover the entire Pentateuch in the course of three years.

Following this there would be a reading from the Prophets. There is no agreement among scholars whether this, too, was prescribed. Then would come normally an explanation and application of one or both of the Scriptures. At the end of the service there would be a blessing by either a priest or a layman.

Scripture would be read in Hebrew, but there would also be a verse-by-verse translation into Aramaic. Custom required the reader to stand; preaching, on the other hand, was done sitting down.

There was no official "minister." An invitation to read and to preach could be extended by the ruling elders to any competent member or even to a visitor. It is also assumed by some commentators that a member or guest could ask for permission to read or preach. My guess is that Jesus had been invited. He was very well-known in the village, had doubtless attended this synagogue often; and there undoubtedly would be great curiosity about the changes that seemed to have taken place in his behavior in the weeks following his baptism. So it seems a very natural thing for him to be asked to read. He is handed the scroll containing the writings of the prophet

Isaiah and unrolls it until he comes to the beginning of the sixty-first chapter. Then he begins to read words describing a postexilic prophet's understanding of his own mission.

It clearly summarizes Jesus' understanding of his ministry as well. Later when agents of John the Baptist came to ask whether Jesus was the person they had been expecting, he described what he had done in the way of healing and preaching in terms which are reminiscent of this passage from Isaiah.

Had not witnesses avowed that the Spirit of the Lord God indeed descended on Jesus at the time of his baptism? Was that not a confirmation of his anointing—his election as the king, the Messiah? Is not his ministry especially directed to relieving the sundry afflictions of those poor in health, status, and wealth, as well as those poor in spirit? Is not the person who receives him and his message especially blessed, another way of saying that he or she is a beneficiary of "the year of the Lord's favour"? There in the synagogue in Nazareth, the messianic age is announced!

In the synagogue there was an aide who did everything from teaching children to punishing criminals. To this aide Jesus returns the Isaiah scroll. Then he sits down. Everyone looks at him intently, expectantly. The atmosphere is one of suspense and, I suspect, one of surprise. Jesus' manner is probably different from what they had previously experienced of him. The mood continues for a little while. People generally hear what they want to hear, and for a time what these people hear fits well with what they desire.

"Today," Jesus says, "in your very hearing this text has come true." *The Messiah has come! These words describe me!*

A synagogue was not like most of our church services where the choir speaks only when spoken to, the minister runs the show, and the people in the congregation are basically silent, allowed only the vehicle of the offering to express their satisfaction or dissatisfaction with what is going on. People talked all the time in synagogue. It was therefore considered a great honor for every eye to be on Jesus and for the people to listen attentively. Now they revert to standard behavior. They "wonder," they speculate, they interpret, they begin to express their true feelings about the preacher—the way people do at coffee hours in our churches.

How is it possible for a man of his birth and education, they ask

themselves, *to speak this way and make such claims about himself?*
Amidst the admiration recorded in the text, one senses that there is
also considerable skepticism and even hostility. "Is not this Joseph's
son?" Since we do not only bear the sins of our fathers, but also a lot
of other baggage people assume we must carry just because they
know our parents ("Like father, like son"), some people in this little
congregation would be certain they have Jesus all figured out because
they have known Joseph and Mary for a long time.

Apparently there is also some envy, some jealousy expressed. Jesus
picks it up. "No doubt you will quote the proverb to me, 'Physician,
heal yourself!', and say, 'We have heard of all your doings at
Capernaum; do the same here in your own home town'." Almost
every culture has a saying equivalent to our "charity begins at home."
The people are distressed, it appears, because they have heard of his
wondrous deeds in the rival town of Capernaum. It is possible to
interpret what is going on here as a demand that Jesus give them a
sign that will confirm that he is who he says he is.

Nothing is clearer in the Gospels than Jesus' total unwillingness to
perform on demand like a magician. The signs are always there, often
in profusion, like seashells on the beach. The eyes of those who expect
to see them will indeed be opened to them. To those willing to entrust
themselves to the Lord without reservation, the signs will come from
time to time to strengthen their faith. Perform miracles on cue?
Never! It is not the signs which persuade, even now. It is the Person or
it is nothing!

So Jesus resists. "I tell you this . . . no prophet is recognized in his
own country."

We need to pause for an additional observation about the text.
Luke alone puts this episode at the beginning of Jesus' ministry. It
makes sense, from one standpoint; what would be more fitting than
for a young man to return to his hometown to mark the beginning of
an important new phase in his life? It would be like saying to the
townspeople, *You helped make me what I have become, and I want to
share the glory and the excitement with you.* This reminds me of how
a boyhood idol of mine, Wendell Willkie, began his presidential
campaign in 1940 in his hometown, Elwood, Indiana. But the
Scripture passage poses problems for scholars because Luke puts
Jesus' ministry in Capernaum after the Nazareth event. What, then,

were the great happenings in Capernaum about which the Nazarenes are jealous? Did Luke get his chronology mixed up? Did he have some special reason for putting this episode where he did in the total story? The truth of the matter is that no one has satisfactory answers to these questions. If total historical factuality is our preoccupation, the gospel may elude us anyway!

In the synagogue Jesus launches off on a review of two stories about the prophets Elijah and Elisha which seems, at first, to have little to do with the issue at hand. The effect on the congregation, however, is to drive them to intense rage. We are left with the impression that what Jesus does is deliberate: he is, really, throwing down a gauntlet so that there will be total clarity about where he stands. What is going on here?

Let us begin with a review of the stories Jesus cites. First is the story about Elijah. In his struggle against the supporters of Baal, Elijah challenges them to put their god into a contest with his. In First Kings, chapter seventeen, the immediate test is to be which of the two gods, Baal or Yahweh, will control the rainfall. We know that Yahweh wins hands down! A drought develops which soon leads to famine. Wherever the holy man goes, however, there is miraculous provision of food. Then the message comes, as even Elijah's special sources seem to dry up, that he is to go to Gentile territory and seek new sources from a Syro-Phoenician widow. Elijah, one needs to remember, is the prophet who most symbolizes resistance to Gentile corruption of the Jewish faith. He has become a powerful folk hero who, legend has it, will be the one to return to usher in the messianic age. So it is shocking to Elijah and to his followers that he is to entrust his welfare to a Gentile, but almost worse is the fact that a Gentile would benefit from the prophet's presence. The widow's stock of flour and oil, we are told in the Old Testament narrative, never runs out. So Jesus is forcing his hearers to remember this "questionable" story about their hero-prophet.

Then he turns to Elijah's heir, Elisha. In Second Kings is the account of his ministry to Naaman, a Syrian general afflicted with leprosy. An Israelite slave girl tells her master that she is sure he can be healed if he will but seek out the prophet; and he goes off with a huge sum of money (probably stolen or otherwise extracted from the Israelites who are currently under Syrian domination) to buy, in his desperation, whatever help he can get. He goes first to the king of Israel with a letter from the king of Syria asking his intercession with Elisha. Israel's king is furious and complains to the prophet that the Syrian king is picking on him again. Elisha calms him and says they should help the general so that he will be aware of the power of Israel's God. The general comes, with all his soldiers and chariots and horses; and Elisha instructs him to wash seven times in the Jordan. The Syrian is enraged at being asked to do anything so silly and prepares to leave. His servants plead with him—they say something akin to "Don't knock it until you've tried it." We know the end of the story—the Syrian soldier bathes, as Elisha orders, and indeed he is healed of his leprosy.

Now, still vivid in the memories of Jesus' listeners is the last serious encounter of their people with the Syrians. In what seemed to be an endless captivity, the Syrians imposed unspeakable atrocities on the Jews. The temple was defamed, and Jews faithful to their God endured not only persecution but often bloody mutilation as well.

The hatred was so intense that the Jews had finally risen up in rebellion. Less than two hundred years before this event in the life of Jesus, the Jews had been led in successful revolt against Syrian oppression by the family of the priest Mattathias. His son, Judas Maccabaeus, led the Israelites to great victories and is still heralded in legend and music. It was a dubious victory at best, however, since the Syrians were soon replaced by another hated oppressor, the Romans.

The memory of Syrian mistreatment rankles the most; the Syrians are, in Jesus' day, still violently hated. For Jesus to emphasize how the great prophets of old had ministered to people outside the household of faith only inflames his hearers until they are ready to do violence against him. This, then, is some of the biblical evidence.

There is, in addition, research by New Testament scholars which helps to explain the intensity of reaction of the people in the Nazareth synagogue. Galilee was a center of the Zealot movement and it is believed that it was especially strong in Nazareth. There were far more Gentiles in Galilee than in Judea, and so there were constant reminders of the extent to which Israel was subject to other peoples and other powers. Nationalist sentiment was, therefore, very intense. In the eyes of many people, the only important issue of Jesus' day would have been "where do you stand on the revolution?" It is very much like the pressure to line up solidly behind Israeli Zionism today. James and John, "the sons of thunder," and Judas are all believed to have been deeply embroiled in the "resistance" movement. It is interesting to speculate that Judas's disillusionment with Jesus may have been caused by His seeming disinterest in the insurrectionist movement. Some have speculated, indeed that Judas's "betrayal" of Jesus may have been designed as a goad to get him on "the right side" of the struggle. Once he saw his life was in danger, surely Jesus would join the revolutionaries.

In any event, it helps to understand why the people in the synagogue are so upset by Jesus' words. Their momentary joy that the Messiah has come is soon destroyed by Jesus' unambiguous assertion that he has come with a message and a ministry intended for all people. He reminds the Jews again that they are a "chosen people" only because of their role in God's particular task. Their being called as a nation is only a means to that end.

So, enraged by the betrayal of their long-expected Messiah, the Jews of Nazareth literally chase him out of town and seek to destroy him by throwing him off a cliff. The Messiah is deemed guilty of blasphemy! But Jesus, whose "hour had not yet come," walks through the crowd and "went away" from Nazareth, probably never to return. He would face such rejection throughout his ministry.

Now we turn to the second half of this composite "event":

> Then he left that place and went away into the territory of Tyre. He found a house to stay in, and he would have liked to remain unrecognized, but this was impossible. Almost at once a woman whose young daughter was possessed by an unclean spirit heard of him, came in, and fell at his feet. (She was a Gentile, a Phoenician of Syria by nationality.) She begged him to drive the spirit out of her daughter. He said to her, "Let the children be satisfied first; it is not fair to take the children's bread and throw it to the dogs." "Sir," she answered, "even the dogs under the table eat the children's scraps." He said to her, "For saying that, you may go home content; the unclean spirit has gone out of your daughter." And when she returned home, she found the child lying in bed; the spirit had left her (Mark 7:24-30).

Some time later, while on a journey through the northern part of the country, deep in "heathen territory," Jesus comes to Tyre. His whole Galilean ministry has not gone well, and he needs some rest, some quiet time, some opportunity to sort out things with his disciples. Surely he could do that in a cosmopolitan city where Jews are few and where there would be minimal curiosity about still another traveler. When one wants to be incognito, one goes to a great city.

Even here, however, people seek him out. His fame has spread even among the Gentiles. A local woman, a Syro-Phoenician by birth and culture, boldly follows him. Her young daughter is demon-possessed. Her faith in Jesus' healing power is such that she pleads for his help.

Matthew's parallel account provides us with some vivid dialogue. The woman says, "Sir! have pity on me, Son of David; my daughter is tormented by a devil." Jesus is silent.

The disciples interpret his silence as a sign of reluctance or disapproval—which possibly it may have been—and they say to him, "Send her away; see how she comes shouting after us." Still there is a recurring pattern; the disciples, time after time, seem determined to "protect" Jesus from people they consider to be unattractive, unpleasant, or demanding.

Now Jesus speaks, and his words sound harsh: "Let the children be satisfied first; it is not fair to take the children's bread and throw it to the dogs." A. M. Hunter has paraphrased it in this way: "'I am a Jew. You know how Jews regard people like you. "Children" and "dogs" is the conventional way of putting it. What have you to say if I put it that way?'"[13]

The woman is really listening. Her desperation is such she cannot afford to get this one wrong. She notes, no doubt with relief, that unlike those other Jews, Jesus is not being insulting. In place of the customary word for "dogs," the word used to describe the vicious, dangerous wild animals that were a great problem for many communities, Jesus uses a gentle diminutive—the word for "little dogs" or "puppies."

Emboldened, the woman says, "Sir, even the dogs under the table eat the children's scraps." *Are you going to deny my child even the crumbs from your table, Lord?* "We are not worthy even to gather up the crumbs from thy table," the prayer of humble access in the

Communion liturgy of the Episcopal Church says, "but thou art the same Lord whose property is always to have mercy."

Whatever his motives—and it is indeed possible that he has to struggle still with the question of whether his mission is to the Jews only or to the whole world or to the Jews first but also to the whole world—Jesus says to the woman, "For saying that, you may go home content; the unclean spirit has gone out of your daughter." That is precisely what the woman discovers when she returns home. Jesus has rewarded the woman's caring boldness, but he has also made a personal decision regarding his own vocation. There is no longer any question about what God has called him to be and do. The woman's great faith in him and the power he possesses from God is the same faith Israel had from time to time expressed and to which it is even here being recalled.

Who belongs? Who is the responsibility of the church? About whom is it the church is to care?

Many people have frequently described their churches as congregations of "like-minded people." At its best, that phrase has meant a fellowship of people who share a commitment to the Lord Jesus and who seek for common ways to express that faith in the world. At its worst, it has meant a fellowship who share the values and prejudices of particular races and classes and cultures to the exclusion of all others. The people in most of our churches look and act and sound very much alike. Our vaunted diversity is expressed far more in separation than in consolidation. We can tolerate our wide range of differences, even celebrate them at denominational gatherings, provided we do not have to spend much time together!

Clear across the spectrum of theological understanding and liturgical practice, Christians these days—as in all days—wrestle with the question of whom to admit. Shall women be ordained? If ordained, shall women be placed in significant leadership positions? (I know of churches that are so divided on this still that they allow women to prepare Communion—that's like "woman's work," after all—but certainly not serve it!) Shall homosexuals be ordained? Shall homosexuals be permitted in our churches? Shall homosexuals even be considered human beings?

As for race . . . Oh, I know there are very few self-confessed racists left in the nation! But it appears to me that there is less contact between blacks and whites in the church now than there was twenty years ago, and maybe less concern about that fact than ever. At dinner parties I hear no less "putting down" of people who are different from us—Hispanics, Orientals, native Americans (whom we still ignorantly insist on calling Indians). The best indicator that attitudes have not changed much is that entire populations and institutions will uproot themselves and move somewhere else in order to avoid welcoming anybody "not like us" into what we still insist on calling "our community."

If you will permit one very personal anguish, how welcome do our churches make the physically handicapped?

So much of our energy goes, even in the church, to keeping people out, to doggedly resisting those who plead or clamor to be let in. Because we do not know them, we fear them; and because we fear them, we tighten security against them. There the walls of partition stand, imprisoning us all.

Jesus came to set the "prisoners" free, to break down the walls of separation, to unite into one great, rich, diverse "nation" all the peoples of the earth. One does not accomplish that easily, not without taking very great risks. To approach a stranger is always to approach the unknown. One cannot assume that all meetings will turn out happily. One must understand that every meeting is at least twice as difficult and fraught with peril as we imagine. After all, there are the other person's fears and prejudices to be overcome as well as our own. The Good News of Jesus is that this victory can happen. Indeed, whenever it does happen, it will be a sign of the presence of the kingdom.

One of my colleagues at New York Seminary is Bob Washington. He is a patient soul, gentle yet tough. He has known the degradation of being black in America; but it has not made him bitter, only realistic. He has signed on for the duration—for the rest of his life—to whittle away at those practices in human society which end up, oddly, demeaning everyone even though they are calculated to demean only some.

When I first met Bob, he was directing an action training/research organization, and early on he invited me to give a lecture on contemporary theology to a group of black clergy. I confess to being more than a little nervous. I had not been with such a group for a couple of years; I knew that relationships between blacks and whites had further deteriorated in that time. I wondered what would happen.

What happened was this: in his introduction, Bob said, "I could tell you all kinds of things about Mel Schoonover, about his schooling, his degrees, his accomplishments. There is really only one thing you need to know about him: Mel is my brother." I am sure there was only brief silence after that statement, but what I heard was the sound of a great explosion as a wall of fear and accumulated misapprehension blew up. There probably cannot be in this culture any more explicit example of the "grace of our Lord Jesus Christ" than for a black man to say of a white man, "He's my brother."

So the question I would have you ponder is, "What if the constituency of the church includes everybody?"

He came again to Nazareth, his hometown, and went, as he was accustomed to do on the sabbath, to the synagogue. He stood up to read the Scripture and was handed the scroll of the prophet Isaiah. He unrolled it until he came to the passage which reads:

> The Spirit of the Lord is upon me because he has anointed
>   me;
> he has sent me to preach good news to the poor,
> to proclaim release to the prisoners and recovery of
>   sight to the blind,
> to heal the brokenhearted,
> to proclaim the year of the Lord's favor and acceptance.

He rolled up the scroll, handed it to the synagogue attendant, and then sat down. Every eye in the place was fixed on him.

"Today," he said, "this prophecy has been fulfilled in your hearing."

There was a stir of approval and admiration in the place; they were surprised that such gracious words should come from his lips. "Isn't this Joseph's son?" they asked.

Then Jesus spoke again, "No doubt you will quote the proverb to me, 'Physician, heal yourself!' and say, 'We have heard of all your doings at Capernaum; do the same here in your hometown.' I tell you this, no prophet is honored in his own country. There were many widows in Israel, you may be sure, in Elijah's time when for three and one-half years there was a drought, and famine held the whole country in its grip; yet it was to none of those that Elijah was sent, but to a widow at Sarepta in the region of Sidon. Also, in the time of the prophet Elisha there were many lepers in Israel, and not one of them was healed, but only Naaman, the Syrian."

At these words, the whole congregation was infuriated. They leapt to their feet, drove him out of the synagogue and the town itself until they came to the edge of the cliff on which the town was built. They meant to throw him over the edge, but he walked straight through that crowd and went on his way.

Then he left that place and later he went into the territory of Tyre. He found a house to stay in, and it was his hope that he would go unrecognized, but this was impossible. Almost at once a woman whose young daughter was possessed by an unclean spirit heard of him, found him, and fell at his feet. (She was a Gentile, a Phoenician of Syria by nationality.) She begged him to heal her child, but he said to her, "Let the children be satisfied first; it is not fair to take the children's bread and throw it to the dogs."

"Sir," she replied, "even the dogs are allowed to have the scraps from the children's table."

He said to her, "For saying that you may go home content; the unclean spirit has gone out of your daughter." And when she returned home, she found the child lying in bed; the spirit had indeed left her.

4
Jericho:
The Poor

H. R. Haldeman and John Mitchell were the twenty-fourth and twenty-fifth persons convicted of Watergate crimes and were sentenced, originally, to terms which could have kept them behind bars for as long as eight years. When they surrendered to authorities, news reports indicated that they both acted as usual: Haldeman, stoic and a bit quizzical; Mitchell, sarcastic and flip. Only after learning that their sentences would be shortened did either man acknowledge that he did anything wrong or felt that he deserved this or any other kind of punishment.

Reading about these two men called to mind one of the people who was convicted and sentenced early because he pleaded guilty. Charles Colson, one of the most unpleasant "public servants" ever inflicted on this nation, has written a moving book, *Born Again*.[14] In it he reports that, feeling very sorry for himself and angry because he was being "persecuted" for doing his job—being obedient to every whim of Richard Nixon—he had gone to see a friend who was helpless to do anything about Colson's fate, but who suggested the two of them "take it to the Lord in prayer." After he had left the friend's home, he had wept for a long time. Various factors doubtless contributed to this uncharacteristic, emotional response. One factor was that he began to see how guilty he was and how he had betrayed values he thought he cherished. Another was that his friend's caring had deeply touched him. A third was that he really felt the presence of God, and it was comforting and sustaining more than it was condemning. He felt he had been born again.

Karl Barth once said that "What man needs is not solution to his problems, but salvation." The ministry of Jesus was very much about salvation. The great irony for people was that he who brought salvation to so many could not save himself.

In our consideration of Jesus' ministry, we find him on his way to Jerusalem for the last time. On his way he passes through the old city of Jericho. Artifacts have been dug up which indicate that there was a community on this site at least eight thousand years ago. Located strategically in the Jordan valley, near an important crossing, it had guarded major trade routes and become a very wealthy and cosmopolitan city.

It was the first major roadblock the children of Israel encountered on their way to the "Promised Land." It was so heavily fortified that Joshua had to resort to superior strategy rather than superior force to destroy it. Not until the time of King Ahab was it fully rebuilt.

Other interesting historical details: One authority says that Jericho was once presented by Mark Anthony as a gift to his mistress, Cleopatra. Herod the Great, at his last breath, ordered the murder of Jericho's foremost Jewish residents so there might be some to mourn his passing vicariously. His son, Archelaeus, rebuilt the magnificent royal palace set in sumptuous gardens, and it is said that in the air over the city lingered the perfume of roses and of balsam—which provided the base for the legendary ointment called Balm of Gilead. Because of its close association with the Herodian family, Jericho was a very influential center in the time of Jesus. Because of its mild climate, it was also a popular resort, especially in winter. Near here, Jesus had been baptized.

Jericho was destroyed again, along with Jerusalem, in the uprising in A.D. 70.

Let us consider now what happened when Jesus passed through Jericho on his way to Jerusalem.

As he approached Jericho a blind man sat at the roadside begging. Hearing a crowd going past, he asked what was happening. They told him, "Jesus of Nazareth is passing by." Then he shouted out, "Jesus, Son of David, have pity on me." The people in front told him to hold his tongue; but he called out all the more, "Son of David, have pity on me." Jesus stopped and ordered the man to be brought to him. When he came up he asked him, "What do you want me to do for you?" "Sir, I want my sight back," he answered. Jesus said to him, "Have back your sight; your faith has cured you." He recovered his sight instantly; and he followed Jesus, praising God. And all the people gave praise to God for what they had seen (Luke 18:35-43).

As Jesus approaches Jericho, a blind beggar sits by the side of the road. Mark provides a name for him: Bartimaeus, son of Timaeus. It is a strategic place to sit, particularly at this time of year. Pilgrims determined to avoid the alternative route through Samaria would be coming by in large numbers on their way to the Passover festival, and they would likely be more responsive to pleas for money. There seems to be an unusual stir, however; an unusually large throng seems to be on the road.

So, curiosity aroused, the blind man asks what is happening. "Jesus of Nazareth is passing by," he is told.

There are many people who assume that those who are in some way physically afflicted are also stupid, but this man is completely alert to what is happening even in his circumscribed world. He has heard about Jesus, heard enough to be persuaded that he is the Messiah. So he cries out, using a messianic title, "Jesus, Son of David, have pity on me!" It is the only time in either Luke or Mark that this title is used.

The handicapped are still barely tolerated in society, and only if they know and keep their place. Again we have an example of people trying to protect Jesus from the very people he came to welcome into the kingdom. The blind man is rebuked by people for crying out. *Hold your tongue,* he is commanded.

The blind man knows this is too good of an opportunity to miss; so he bellows out, "Son of David, have pity on me!" Jesus stops.

Mark attempts to redeem the disciples' reputations by then having them say to the beggar, "Take heart; stand up; he is calling you."

Bring him here, Jesus orders. Bartimaeus, according to Mark, throws off his cloak, jumps to his feet, and begins walking toward Jesus.

Be careful, Bartimaeus. You may stumble and fall. Remember you are blind.

Be careful, be damned! I am a blind man desperate to be healed. So there he is, standing before Jesus. "What do you want me to do for you?" Jesus asks. There is an echo here of the question he had asked before of the infirm and crippled: "Do you want to be healed?"

"Sir," the blind man answers, "I want my sight back."

"Have your sight back," Jesus says; "your faith has cured you." Here I wonder if the King James Version is not more meaningful than our more "accurate" modern translations when it says, "Thy faith hath *saved* thee" (italics added).

"Cured" or "saved," the man can see once more. In the ecstasy of that new life—for who would be bold enough to say that this man has not been born again—he follows Jesus into the town, thanking God for what has happened. His witness is so compelling in so many ways that the people around him join in their own acts and words of praise.

If anything like that happened in my ministry, I would live on the excited memory of it for months. This, however, was but a prelude to still—in many ways—a more dramatic recovery of sight. Let us return to the account in Luke's Gospel:

> Entering Jericho he made his way through the city. There was a man there named Zacchaeus; he was superintendent of taxes and very rich. He was eager to see what Jesus looked like; but, being a little man, he could not see him for the crowd. So he ran on ahead and climbed a sycamore-tree in order to see him, for he was to pass that way. When Jesus came to the place, he looked up and said, "Zacchaeus, be quick and come down; I must come and stay with you today." He climbed down as fast as he could and welcomed him gladly. At this there was a general murmur of disapproval. "He has gone in," they said, "to be the guest of a sinner." But Zacchaeus stood there and said to the Lord, "Here and now, sir, I give half my possessions to charity; and if I have cheated anyone, I am ready to repay him four times over." Jesus said to him, "Salvation has come to this house today!—for this

man too is a son of Abraham, and the Son of Man has come to seek and save what is lost" (Luke 19:1-10).

There is a man, we are told, by the name of Zacchaeus, who lived in Jericho. Ironically, his name means "pure" or "righteous." This is ironic because he is anything but pure or righteous. Tax collectors, in that time, were by definition crooks. His thievery might almost be legitimate, but it was thievery nonetheless. One apparently bought the privilege of being tax collector, much as one would now buy a hamburger franchise. In this instance, one's intent would not be to line one's stomach with two-all-beef-patties-special-sauce-lettuce-cheese-pickles-onions-on-a-sesame-seed-bun but to line one's pockets with money. Let us not miss the significance of the description of Zacchaeus's success: Zacchaeus is "very rich."

He pays a great price, as many do, for his wealth. He is despised by other citizens. We are told that he is a little man (although the text is not conclusive; it may be Jesus who was the little man) and could not see Jesus as he passed because of the crowd. I have an idea that Zacchaeus, despite his wealth and power, does not want to risk forcing his way through a crowd that would know him all too well and could hardly be expected to be friendly. After all, it is easy to make body contact in a large crowd; and not all body contact is pleasant.

Undaunted, determined, needful, Zacchaeus runs ahead and climbs up onto the wide-spreading branches of a low-growing sycamore tree (described in one reference book as a type of wild fig tree). Here he is sure to catch a glimpse of Jesus, because apparently it is the only route through the town.

When Jesus gets there, he looks up and calls out, "Zacchaeus, be quick and come down; I must come and stay with you today." Zacchaeus scurries down from his perch and embraces Jesus.

People looking on begin to express their disapproval. *Doesn't he know who this evil man is? Is he going to have a meal with this sinner? Shame!*

Of course Jesus knows who Zacchaeus is. If he had not known, it would have been no trouble to ask someone who that funny little man in the tree might be, and it would be equally natural for people to give him a vivid, if brief, identification. Surely it is not necessary for Jesus to be conscious of everything, even this man's name, as some traditionalist interpreters have claimed. We can only speculate what Zacchaeus's motives had been for this undignified behavior, but surely there is no question of Jesus' motives. He boldly invites himself to Zacchaeus's house. Francis of Assisi once said, "God is always courteous and does not invade the privacy of the human soul." True, but he knows where he will be welcome, and it is at that door that he knocks.

In any event this story is much like those in Luke and Mark about the encounter of Jesus and Levi. Both Levi and Zacchaeus belonged to the despised class of tax collectors. In both instances Jesus scandalizes pious Jews by accepting the hospitality of people they consider outcasts. He was always scandalizing pious folk by consorting with sinners, even as now he still scandalizes pious folk who think that the gospel is for the righteous or perhaps for the self-righteous—as indeed it is.

In his joy, Zacchaeus has the courage to face his critics. To Jesus he says, "Here and now, sir, I give half my possessions to charity; and if I have cheated anyone, I am ready to repay him four times over." That's what the Roman law required as restitution for theft; Jewish law required the same, but only after conviction. Voluntary restitution, as in this case, would have required only a 20 percent penalty.

Jesus says, "Salvation has come to this house today!" In what appears to be an editorial "explanation," Jesus seems to defend his action by reminding his hearers that Zacchaeus is "one of us," is a son of Abraham—a Jew. Or can it be that Jesus is reminding us that the real standard for being a son of Abraham is not birth at all but is that one have enough faith in the living God that he or she is willing to move on to another country—of residence *or* behavior? Then he concludes with what is a coda for his ministry: ". . . the Son of Man has come to seek and save what is lost." No one, despite his riches, had been more lost than Zacchaeus!

The great Russian writer, Turgenev, said that the face of Jesus is "like all men's faces," by which I understand he meant that each person can see something of himself or herself in the face of our Lord. In a similar way Lloyd Douglas interpreted this story: "Zacchaeus," said the carpenter gently, "what did you see that made you desire this peace?" "Good master—I saw—mirrored in your eyes—the face of the Zacchaeus I was meant to be!"[15]

The cities of America are rapidly becoming the dormitories for the very rich and the very poor. The "great American dream," some say, is still for the middle class to flee the creeping blight of the city to the homogenized communities of suburbia. The rich can afford to avoid the blight. The poor have no recourse.

What problems the poor in America face! They are not made more tolerable by comparing them with the plight of the poor elsewhere. I live ten blocks north of a social "Maginot Line" in Manhattan above which most people live in poverty. Below that line is the so-called "silk-stocking district" where New Yorkers live in unbelievable luxury. It makes it hard to accept being poor when, before your eyes, people flaunt their wealth. If the looting mobs of our last blackout had penetrated beyond that geographic and social line, there is certainty that the police would have used violence.

The poor in my city and in this country die sooner and are subject to more debilitating illnesses before their deaths. They have less to eat than the rest of us. They are poorly housed. They "serve time" in educational institutions staffed to a large extent by people who do not expect them to learn. They are more likely to "get in trouble," and for them justice is delayed if it is ever achieved. Somehow a myth has grown up in this country that the poor have an almost ideal life—they don't work, they propagate babies, and the rest of us pay their bills. This is pure myth. There are a few who manage to exploit the welfare system, to have a comfortable existence, or, rarely, even to get rich. For the masses of the poor—that 20 percent of our society who are really outside or (at best) on the fringes of the money economy—the preoccupation of life is survival. In that struggle, some vow to accomplish it even at the expense of someone else's survival.

That is not to say that the rich are not engaged in a similar struggle. Someone once described being rich as being imprisoned in a golden cage. Clearly the struggle is at a different level. Camus has a character in one of his books say that the rich are unable to stave off death, but they are often able to buy some time. If the poor are both poor in this world's goods and also often poor in spirit, the rich are often troubled with spiritual poverty. So many of them, the press would have us believe, are restlessly seeking something in their rounds of parties and even in their sponsorship of good causes. The rich virtually alone support the psychiatric establishment.

That leads me to wonder if the church does not use the keys of the kingdom to bind both the rich and the poor in our society. As an institution made up largely of middle class people, it seems to me that we deprecate the poor even as we are much in awe of the rich. We admire the rich, we envy them, and not uncommonly we fawn before them when they join our churches. We allow them sometimes to purchase, through their large pledges, a bit of almost sincere approval. We encourage their myth that riches are a sign of divine favor (a defensibly Judaic, a questionably Christian doctrine), even when those riches have been amassed in violation and contradiction of everything the gospel holds dear. Suppose that what the rich need is to be released from the bondage of guilt just like the rest of us. Suppose what they need to hear most urgently is that they, too, are sinners and that, like Zacchaeus, they need to make restitution for that portion of their fortune garnered through exploitation and theft. Jesus said that it was harder for a rich man to enter the kingdom than for a camel to go through the eye of a needle. That must be true. The rich can constantly be beguiled with the notion that their bank accounts can buy them immunity, and the church reinforces that by minimizing their need for salvation in exchange for maximizing their gifts.

So both the rich and the poor need redemption. Both desperately need to hear and experience the good news that God is on the side of us all. Both the Bartimaeuses and the Zacchaeuses of this world need recovery of sight and the discovery of a vision of life which will enable them to leave the past behind and, joyfully, to follow Jesus.

For the body of Christ in the world—the church—there are, it seems to me, some fairly obvious consequences. In relation to the poor, I suspect, it means once again personalizing charity. One of the reasons we get so hung up in our notions of who the poor are, what they are like, and whether they "deserve" what they get (both positively and negatively!) is that we have erected very effective buffers between us and the poor. Since charity is now almost always channeled through vast structures of relief, the poor have become faceless and remote, and the helping relationship has become very impersonal. The increasing crisis facing the aged in our society may, strangely, turn out to be a form of blessing for society if it can help us become conscious again of particular people with particular imaginable and manageable problems. If we can recover some of the sense of personal need, it may make us both more receptive to, but also more responsible for, large-scale programs when they become necessary.

It may also mean a difference in how we raise and spend our "benevolence" money. It may mean that such aid for those beyond the immediate "family" will come to be seen not just as something that comes out of our surplus, but something which *must* be raised simply because there is need which conscience will not permit us to ignore. Material from a pulpit committee which came to my attention recently seemed to boast that this church did not engage in special fund raising but relied on pledges and designated offerings for everything it did. Well, maybe they should engage in fund-raising projects. Maybe there are some human needs which can only be met by our extending ourselves or even overextending ourselves and doing more than we "budgeted."

There is one more thing. The church neglects healing at its own peril. Salvation is surely a state of wholeness in which body, mind, and spirit—to use a familiar biblical trinity—are in some state of harmony. Broken bodies, broken spirits, and broken relationships all need to be healed. The resurgence of interest in and practice of healing ministries is one of the more hopeful things in the church these days. Obviously such ministries carry great risks. The potential for fakery and fraud is great. Medical science continues to be a major focus of the healing arts for the church. Yet we flirt also with a risk there—the risk of making an idol of a profession that sometimes is guilty of rendering genuine hurt as well as genuine help. As Kenneth Clark said about education and teachers and Dwight Eisenhower said about defense and generals: healing is too important to be left entirely to doctors. Perhaps prayer might begin to assume more reality and power among us if, once again, it were focused on relieving specific human ills. Do not be disappointed if healing exactly as you asked for does not come. Sometimes it comes in other forms which are more profound than we ever dare to hope.

All well and good, but what of ministry to the rich? If mercy gets emphasized more with the poor, I suspect justice must be the dominant theme for the rich. One of the richest men I know—rich enough to give away 90 percent of his current income—talked with me a while back about a telephone conversation with his accountant. He was struck, he said, by the irony of the situation. "My accountant was explaining to me how he had figured out a way to save me money on my taxes—a sum larger than I suspect he earns in an entire year." My friend has resolved this irony to a point by struggling to give his money away responsibly so that it can improve the quality of life and opportunity for others. I wish I could say that his church had encouraged him to act in this fashion, but it has been characteristically silent.

It *does* matter how people make their money. Money is not a neutral commodity if it is produced by human or ecological rape. It *does* matter if people are wasteful even if they can "afford it." Obesity cannot be defended in a world where some die of starvation. It *does* matter how people invest their money, if the resulting gain is at the expense of someone else's loss. Financial gain is obscene if it results in the continuing enslavement of blacks or Latin Americans or native Americans—those people we describe with the ironic word "underdeveloped." It *does* matter how we spend our money—do we build the human community or tear it down?

I realize that I am now "meddling"! People tell me that it is nobody's business how they earn their money or how they spend it. They tell me that the church has no business being involved in economic or political issues, which is only a covert way of saying that the church has no business sticking its nose into their affairs. Maybe it does. The church knows, when it is the church, that nothing belongs to us. Everything belongs to God, and we are at best mere stewards of his estate! The model once again is Jesus the Christ who, though rich, made himself poor. "Bearing the human likeness . . . he humbled himself, and in obedience accepted even death—death on a cross. Therefore God raised him to the heights and bestowed on him the name above all names, that at the name of Jesus every knee should bow—in heaven, on earth, and in the depths—and every tongue confess, 'Jesus Christ is Lord,' to the glory of God the Father" (Philippians 2:8-11).

We all, rich or poor, are sinners in the sight of God. We all, rich or poor, can be saved by grace. We can experience the salvation of the Lord which frees us from unnecessary blindness, which rids us of the need of "taking care of Number One," which lays before us a picture of a redeemed world and invites us to share in its creation.

Who will offer people that opportunity? Will it be the church? What if the church's real task is to decide if it loves people—rich or poor—enough to extend God's salvation to all?

As Jesus approached Jericho on his way to Jerusalem for celebration of the Passover, a blind beggar sat along the side of the road. Hearing the footsteps and voices of many people, he asked what was happening; and he was told that Jesus of Nazareth was passing by. Then he shouted, "Jesus, Son of David, have pity on me." People told him to be quiet, but he shouted all the louder, "Son of David, have pity on me."

Jesus stopped and ordered that the man be brought to him. When they stood face to face, Jesus asked, "What do you want me to do for you?"

"Sir, I want my sight restored," the blind man replied.

"It is restored! Your faith has cured you." And the man suddenly could see again, and he followed Jesus down the road praising God for what had happened. And all the people did likewise.

Entering Jericho, Jesus made his way through the city. There was a man there named Zacchaeus, who was the chief tax collector and who had grown very rich. He was eager to see what Jesus looked like; but, being a little man, he could not see him because of the crowd. So he ran ahead and climbed into a sycamore tree in order to get a better view, for he knew Jesus had to come that way.

When Jesus got to that spot, he looked up and said, "Zacchaeus, be quick and come down from there, for I must come and stay with you today." Zacchaeus climbed down as fast as he could and welcomed Jesus with open arms.

At this there was a general murmur of disapproval from onlookers. "He has gone in," they said, "to be the guest of a sinner."

But Zacchaeus stood his ground and said to the Lord, "Here and now I give half of everything I own to the poor; and if I have cheated anyone, I will repay him fourfold."

Jesus said to him, "Salvation has come to this house today! This man is a son of Abraham. The Son of Man has come to seek and save what is lost."

5

Jerusalem:

Politics

At last, like Jesus, we come to Jerusalem—*the* Holy City for much of the world's population. It is a city whose streets have been filled with laughter and joyous expectation for thousands of years. It is a city whose streets also have run with blood and have been filled with laments for centuries. Jerusalem is a city from which many people have never been able to bear separation.

It has been there for at least 6,000 years. There are written records concerning it for 3,500 years. It is believed to be the Salem whose king was Melchizedek, mentioned in Genesis. David is thought to have conquered it from the Jebusites 3,000 years ago. Imagine one city playing a significant role in every fluctuation of a nation's history for three millenia! That's how old Jerusalem is; that's how important Jerusalem is.

Our spiritual ancestors have had an intense love affair with Jerusalem. The Jews were always singing about it, whether in sadness or gladness. When in exile, the psalmist wrote,

> By the rivers of Babylon we sat down and wept
> when we remembered Zion. . . .

> If I forget you, O Jerusalem,
>   let my right hand wither away;
> let my tongue cling to the roof of my mouth
>   if I do not remember you,
> if I do not set Jerusalem
>   above my highest joy.
>
>   Psalm 137:1, 5-6

In happier times, another writer said,

> Now we stand within your gates, O Jerusalem:
> Jerusalem that is built to be a city where people
>   come together in unity;
> to which the tribes resort, the tribes of the Lord,
>   to give thanks to the Lord himself,
>   the bounden duty of Israel.
> For in her are set the thrones of justice,
>   the thrones of the house of David.
> Pray for the peace of Jerusalem;
>   "May those who love you prosper;
> peace be within your ramparts
>   and prosperity in your palaces.
>
>   Psalm 122:2-7

It was this Jerusalem, Luke tells us, that Jesus beheld and wept. "If only you had known, on this great day, the way that leads to peace!" The early church believed that this was a prediction of the destruction of Jerusalem in A.D. 70. Perhaps on that occasion Jesus wept merely for the hard-hearted rulers of the city, Jew and Roman alike, who persisted in subjecting people to the ways of violence rather than allowing them to know peace; perhaps he wept for the simple, innocent folk who do not, ever, deserve to be so victimized; and—perhaps—he wept for himself. On this "great day," the time of his "triumphal entry" into the Holy City, Jesus rides "in majesty, in lowly pomp ride on to die . . ."

Let us turn to the account of that event in the Gospel According to John:

> The next day the great body of pilgrims who had come to the festival, hearing that Jesus was on the way to Jerusalem, took palm branches and went out to meet him, shouting, "Hosanna! Blessings on him who comes in the name of the Lord! God bless the king of Israel!" Jesus found a donkey and mounted it, in

accordance with the text of Scripture: "Fear no more, daughter of Zion; see, your king is coming, mounted on an ass's colt." At the time his disciples did not understand this, but after Jesus had been glorified they remembered that this had been written about him, and that this had happened to him. The people who were present when he called Lazarus out of the tomb and raised him from the dead told what they had seen and heard. That is why the crowd went to meet him; they had heard of this sign that he had performed. The Pharisees said to one another, "You see you are doing no good at all; why, all the world has gone after him!" (John 12:12-19).

What a day it is! For the Synoptic Gospels, this is another "homecoming"—Jesus' first visit to Jerusalem since he had begun his ministry three years before. John pictures him having been there several times. This visit is different, however; Jesus has just raised Lazarus from the dead in the presence of Galilean pilgrims on their way to the capital to celebrate the Passover. They have preceded him there and, in their enthusiasm, have aroused people to fever-pitch excitement about this remarkable man who can even overcome the power of death. It so upsets the authorities that they vow to kill both Jesus and Lazarus.

John's Gospel alone pictures people as coming out from Jerusalem to greet Jesus. As a sign that they desire him to be their king and are indeed prepared to give him open public support, they hail him as a royal hero by the traditional act of waving branches of palm. Even as the people in John 6 had misunderstood the feeding of the five thousand, so the contemporary Jesuit scholar Raymond Brown says they have misunderstood the raising of Lazarus. They still are determined that Jesus shall be a traditional warrior king, ridding them of foreign oppressors and restoring the grandeur of Israel's ancient monarchy.

As they come, they shout "Hosanna!" which means "Save now!" "Blessings on him who comes in the name of the Lord"—that is, who comes bearing the power of God. "God bless the King of Israel!" *Jesus, you must be our king!*

Luke tells us that the religious authorities demand that Jesus rebuke the people and tell them to be silent. They want to avoid anything that will upset their Roman rulers. Jesus refuses and says, *If these should hold their peace, the stones would cry out!*

Again John diverges from the Synoptic traditions. The other Gospel writers portray Jesus sending his disciples to get a donkey on which no one has yet ridden. (For the Jews there was almost a quality of sacredness attached to newness. This explains in the Old Testament the emphasis on first fruits, the new moon, the first year of married life. This explains in the life of Jesus the emphasis on the newness of the donkey, the newness of the tomb in which he is buried, the newness of the linen which enwraps his body.) In John, however, Jesus mounts a donkey which is "found," apparently grazing by the road. Obviously Jesus is attempting to convey some important message to the people by means of this particular symbolism.

Raymond Brown argues that it refers to the witness of the prophet Zephaniah,[16] who pictured the king as a gift to all the peoples of the earth, not to Israel's nationalistic glory. Traditionally the church has turned to another prophet for interpretation. Zechariah had pictured a king who was both victorious and humble, one who came not as a military conqueror but as a man of peace. Moffatt translates the pertinent description this way:

> Here comes your King,
> triumphant and victorious,
> riding humbly on an ass,
> on the foal of an ass!
> He banishes all chariots from Ephraim,
> war-horses from Jerusalem,
> and battle bows;
> his words make peace for nations,
> his sway extends from sea to sea,
> from the Euphrates to the ends of earth.
> Zechariah 9:9-10

Everyone present on this day feels strong emotions. The disciples are bewildered, according to John, and do not understand until much later what is happening. Only then do they comprehend this strange act of humility, that all along Jesus intends to be this kind of king. The people are ecstatic; the man who could raise Lazarus from the grave obviously is invincible. The religious authorities, determined to sacrifice Jesus in order that the nation as they know it might survive, at this juncture are in deep gloom. All their carefully wrought plans

seem to be collapsing. "You see ... all the world has gone after him!"
Soon the picture changes radically.

From Caiaphas Jesus was led into the Governor's headquarters. It was now early morning, and the Jews themselves stayed outside the headquarters to avoid defilement, so that they could eat the Passover meal. So Pilate went out to them and asked, "What charge do you bring against this man?" "If he were not a criminal," they replied, "we should not have brought him before you." Pilate said, "Take him away and try him by your own law." The Jews answered, "We are not allowed to put any man to death." Thus they ensured the fulfilment of the words by which Jesus had indicated the manner of his death.

Pilate then went back into his headquarters and summoned Jesus. "Are you the king of the Jews?" he asked. Jesus said, "Is that your own idea, or have others suggested it to you?" "What! am I a Jew?" said Pilate. "Your own nation and their chief priests have brought you before me. What have you done?" Jesus replied, "My kingdom does not belong to this world. If it did, my followers would be fighting to save me from arrest by the Jews. My kingly authority comes from elsewhere." "You are a king, then?" said Pilate. Jesus answered, "King" is your word. My task is to bear witness to the truth. For this was I born; for this I came into the world, and all who are not deaf to truth listen to my voice." Pilate said, "What is truth?" and with those words went out again to the Jews. "For my part," he said, "I find no case against him. But you have a custom that I release one prisoner for you at Passover. Would you like me to release the king of the Jews?" Again the clamour rose: "Not him; we want Barabbas!" (Barabbas was a bandit.)

Pilate now took Jesus and had him flogged; and the soldiers plaited a crown of thorns and placed it on his head, and robed him in a purple cloak. Then time after time they came up to him, crying, "Hail, King of the Jews!" and struck him on the face.

Once more Pilate came out and said to the Jews, "Here he is; I am bringing him out to let you know that I find no case against him"; and Jesus came out, wearing the crown of thorns and the purple cloak. "Behold the Man!" said Pilate. The chief priests

and their henchmen saw him and shouted, "Crucify! crucify!"
"Take him and crucify him yourselves," said Pilate; "for my part
I find no case against him." The Jews answered, "We have a law;
and by that law he ought to die, because he has claimed to be Son
of God."

When Pilate heard that, he was more afraid than ever, and
going back into his headquarters he asked Jesus, "Where have
you come from?" But Jesus gave him no answer. "Do you refuse
to speak to me?" said Pilate. "Surely you know that I have
authority to release you, and I have authority to crucify you?"
"You would have no authority at all over me," Jesus replied, "if it
had not been granted you from above; and therefore the deeper
guilt lies with the man who handed me over to you."

From that moment Pilate tried hard to release him; but the
Jews kept shouting, "If you let this man go, you are no friend to
Caesar; any man who claims to be a king is defying Caesar."
When Pilate heard what they were saying, he brought Jesus out
and took his seat on the tribunal at the place known as "The
Pavement" ("Gabbatha" in the language of the Jews). It was the
eve of Passover, about noon. Pilate said to the Jews, "Here is
your king." They shouted, "Away with him! Away with him!
Crucify him!" "Crucify your king?" said Pilate. "We have no
king but Caesar," the Jews replied. Then at last, to satisfy them,
he handed Jesus over to be crucified (John 18:28–19:16).

Now, less than a week after his triumphant arrival in Jerusalem,
Jesus is arrested, tried first before the Sanhedrin and the chief priests,
and condemned for blasphemy—for being an enemy of God. During
this trial Simon Peter—the "rock" on which the church was to be
built—has crumbled into sand. *You were a follower of his, weren't
you?*

No, I don't know him at all.

Early in the morning, around six, according to John's chronology,
Jesus is taken to appear before Pontius Pilate, the Roman governor.
Accompanying him, we are told, are at least some of the members of
the Sanhedrin, the chief priests, and temple security guards. In John,
at least, there is absolutely no substantiation of the traditional Good
Friday sermon which has been preached from countless pulpits.

These are *not* the same people who on the previous Sunday had shouted "Hosanna!" As the masses of citizens generally are, most of Jesus' supporters are totally ignorant of what is happening; and when they do become informed, they find themselves helpless to do anything.

Most of the people accompanying Jesus, then, will soon be presiding over the most sacred ceremonies in the nation's religious life. The priests among them will slaughter the lambs for the Passover. They *must not* become contaminated, for rites of purification could take anywhere from twenty-four hours to a week. Do they consider contact with all Gentiles contaminating? Is it the assumed presence of leavened bread in a Gentile's house they fear? No one knows for sure the source of their anxiety that they might be defiled. Clearly it is not the murder of an innocent man that they fear will contaminate them! That rarely troubles the conscience of either church or state. Whatever it is, they stop outside the palace where the Roman governor is holding court; and Pilate, as eager as they to maintain the peace, agrees to come out to meet them.

The most ancient of Christian creeds still in common use in the church immortalizes Pilate—our Lord "suffered under Pontius Pilate." Who *was* Pontius Pilate?

Judea, where he was procurator from A.D. 26–36, was considered a minor post in the Empire; and Pilate deserved no better. He had low rank and social status. Philo pictured him as a corrupt and cruel man. Josephus wrote vividly of his blunders and atrocities, chief among them his tendency to be rash and to overreact to situations. John—indeed the whole New Testament—pictures Pilate more sympathetically. In Jesus' trial he, at least, seems to make an effort to maintain proper judicial process and appears genuinely to desire Jesus' release. The Jewish authorities have his number, so to speak; they know how basically weak, insecure, and petty he is. They know he fears the emperor—the moody, jealous, suspicious, ferocious Tiberias—far more than he fears either them or God.

"What charge do you bring against this man?" he demands to know. He undoubtedly already knows. After all, he has been a party to the whole matter, providing soldiers to detain Jesus; and his readiness to try the case at dawn suggests to some people advance information. It appears that his intent is to remind the Jews that he is an officer of Rome and to insist that proper procedure be followed. The Jews are evasive. Their response seems to be surprise and annoyance: *If he were not a criminal, we would not have handed him over to you.* Previously John has used "handed him over" to refer to Judas' betrayal; now the onus of betrayal is passed on to the Jewish authorities.

Pilate gets in his second "dig": "Take him away and try him by your own law." (Recent studies have shown that indeed Roman law was binding on the governor only in relation to Roman citizens and in Roman cities, but that the practice was for the governor to keep in his own hands all essential powers on which the maintenance of order depended.)

Some scholars want to take this at face value and defend Pilate as being ignorant of the facts—he does not know the limits of the Jews' power. Others say he is only standing on due process of law and stating that he cannot conduct a trial in the absence of a charge and proper evidence. Still others—and I endorse this position—say he was being sarcastic.

Pilate goes inside and summons Jesus. *You are the "king" of the Jews, I take it.* The charge, if proved, could lead to condemnation for blasphemy before the religious court or for high treason before Pilate. Clearly it is the charge the Jews hope to substantiate.

Jesus parries: "Is this your own idea, or have others suggested it to you?"

Pilate sneers: "Am I a Jew?" If he believed in a deity, one can imagine that Pilate would have quickly added, "God forbid!"

The interrogation continues. *Your own religious authorities have brought you here and seem determined to have you killed.* "What have you done?"

Jesus seeks to persuade Pilate that his kingdom is not of earthly origin or political in character, as Pilate would understand politics. Earthly kings have armies to fight for them, but Jesus stands undefended before the governor. "My kingly authority comes from elsewhere."

"You are a king, then," Pilate interjects. Jesus does not deny it but indicates that it is not a title he would choose spontaneously to describe his role. In any event, he is a king only for those who recognize, acknowledge, and affirm the authority of truth. Pilate quickly asks with loud resignation, "What is truth?" John would say that is the wrong question. Rather, the question is, "Who is truth?" For John the answer is crystal clear: it is Jesus who incarnates truth. The weak, cynical, bored Roman has been touched by Jesus and goes out to say that he can find no reason to hold him. Rather than being decisive and releasing Jesus, Pilate seems to devise a plan designed to get the Jews to authorize him to do so. He refers to the custom of releasing someone from prison in a limited amnesty on significant feast days, with the people choosing the prisoner. "Would you like me to release the king of the Jews?"

Pilate has bungled. If he seeks to win their clemency for Jesus, to call him their king is not the way to do it. He grossly underestimates not only their hatred for our Lord, but also their shrewdness in analyzing what he was doing. So they cry out, "Not him; we want Barabbas!" In the terse, pregnant manner characteristic of Scripture, John records, "Barabbas was a bandit."

Who was Barabbas? There are no historical references to him outside the New Testament. "Bandit" normally would have been used to describe someone who preyed on travelers, who relied on stealth rather than violence, a mugger more than a murderer. Josephus used the word, however, to describe people who combined robbery and warfare. It is a term, some scholars say, used frequently in relation to the Zealots. The Synoptic Gospels clearly present Barabbas as a revolutionary. His imprisonment and the interest people had in it may mean that he was the leader of a recent insurrection in the city. Matthew described him as notorious, the same word Josephus used to describe the Zealot leaders. If he had in fact committed murder, no pardon should have been permitted under Jewish law. But history amply documents that even murder can be excused if it is deemed to be an act of patriotism rather than an act of crime.

Raymond Brown speculates that the two "thieves" crucified with Jesus were other revolutionaries, and that Barabbas, too, was under sentence of death. So the Jewish leaders see a way of accomplishing several things in one act. They can enhance their credibility with the general populace by asking release of a popular hero. They can embarrass the Roman governor by forcing him either to release a person already identified as a danger to. the domestic tranquility which Pilate is supposed to maintain at all costs or to violate his social contract with them to release a prisoner of their choice. Finally, it enables them to settle their score with Jesus. "Not him; we want Barabbas!"

Pilate then orders Jesus to be whipped. Scourging was usually preliminary to crucifixion. Done with an iron-tipped and iron-weighted lash, it tore the flesh to ribbons, often causing immediate death. Crucifixion damaged no vital parts of the body. Death could take a long time—suffocation, exposure, fatigue, hunger, thirst: these are not quick causes of death. The whipping was designed to speed death; and it seems clear that Jesus was badly hurt by it, since he lasted barely three hours on the cross.

Picking up their cues from Pilate's manner, the soldiers begin to mock Jesus. *We have a king here, do we? Well, a king should be properly dressed.* The robe or cloak which they put on him was probably a faded red, since purple dye (from shellfish) was very expensive. The crown of thorns was reminiscent of the garland of laurel leaves worn by their own emperor. Now dressed like a "king," Jesus is slapped and pushed around and subjected to the ridicule of a parody of the salute they were accustomed to giving Caesar ("Ave Caesar").

Pilate brings this bleeding, humiliated figure before the Jewish leaders saying, *Ecce Homo*—"Behold the Man!" What an enigmatic statement this is. Is it a statement designed to elicit sympathy from the Jews? Is it intended to emphasize the ridiculousness of taking such a hapless figure seriously? Is it designed to show Pilate's contempt in order to goad the crowd into demanding release of Jesus? Is it a way of saying, "Here is a man, a *real* man"?

The hearts of the chief priests and elders of the faith are unmoved. They shout all the louder that Jesus be crucified. Again Pilate's desire to release Jesus is thwarted. In apparent anger and pique, he snarls that they should take Jesus and execute him themselves, knowing full well they have no authority to do so and that it is ritually unthinkable. *I find no reason to condemn him. He is no threat to Rome.* Alarmed, the Jews cry out that Jesus has violated their law. Threat to Rome or not, Jesus was a threat to them because he had claimed to be the Son of God.

John tells us now what has been holding back Pilate all along. He has the legal authority to release Jesus, he has the troops to enforce his decision, but he is afraid. Once the Jewish leaders perceive that, there is no way Jesus can be spared; for someone who is scared can rather easily be persuaded that the highest value in the situation is to save one's own skin. Before this, Pilate may have been scared that another insurrection, such as the one for which Barabbas was imprisoned, was brewing, one which might not be so easily contained, for Jesus is surely a more popular figure than Barabbas overall. Now, however, his curiosity has been aroused, and he confronts Jesus with the question, "Where have you come from?" *Are you a god?*

Weak from the beating he has had, Jesus does not even have the energy to respond. "Do you refuse to speak to me? Surely you know that I have authority to release you, and I have authority to crucify you?"

Jesus musters his waning physical resources. "You would have no authority at all over me . . . if it had not been granted you from above. . . ." *Your power, Pilate, does not come from the emperor but from God. Even you are not as guilty of what is happening here as the ones who have handed me over to you. They are my own people!*

From that time on, John says, Pilate frantically searches for some way to free Jesus. The Jewish authorities know they have him where they want him and they proceed to administer the *coup de grace.* "If you let this man go, you are no friend to Caesar; any man who claims to be a king is defying Caesar." *You just wait until we get through with you in Rome, Pilate. Just let us get word to the emperor how you have vacillated in an open-and-shut case of threat to national security and how you managed to alienate the leaders of the country who have worked so hard to keep things calm and under control. You have even protected someone who claims to be a rival to the emperor. Let us see how long you retain your appointment after that! Everyone knows how ruthless Tiberias is with people he considers disloyal.*

Pilate's resistance is broken.

The ceremonial "pavement" is laid out in front of Pilate, from which the governor traditionally pronounces sentence—*ibis in crucem*—you shall go to the cross. He can order any form of execution, including the customary Jewish stoning. The Jews want crucifixion because they believe it will disgrace Jesus. It is considered the same as hanging, and the Law says "a hanged man is accursed in the sight of God."

It is now about noon. Pilate has one last barb to throw. "Here is your king," he solemnly announces.

"Crucify him!"

"Crucify your king?"

Then, in their joyous frenzy, the Jews respond, "We have no king but Caesar."

Did you hear that, King David? Those centuries of waiting for a king to come from your house and lineage were all in vain. "We have no king but Caesar!"

"Then at last, to satisfy them, he handed Jesus over to be crucified."

Anti-Semites, who are covertly with us always, have seized upon this account to justify their attacks on the Jews. Pilate wanted to release Jesus, but the Jews were so implacable in their hatred of Jesus that they forced him to have the Christ put to death. Unspeakable atrocities have been inflicted on Jews through the centuries, justified as acts of vengeance for the greatest atrocity of all. Whatever truth or half-truth there may be in such interpretations, whoever gave such people the right to play God?

John does portray Pilate more sympathetically than the other Gospels. One needs to remember, however, that Pilate had both the power and the opportunity to free Jesus, but he did not. How that can absolve Pilate from guilt escapes me. No one tried to save Jesus—not the disciples, not the crowds who cheered him during the triumphal entry, no one.

Johann Heerman, reflecting on these events centuries later, asked:

> Who was the guilty?
> Who brought this upon thee?

His answer is one which has resonated with sensitive Christians through two thousand years:

> Alas, my treason,
> Jesus, hath undone thee!
> 'Twas I, Lord Jesus,
> I it was denied thee;
> I crucified thee.[17]

Who is to blame for Jesus' death? We all are!

During the early years of my pastorate in East Harlem, the

people of Chambers Church were always picketing for one thing or another. This time it was for the installation of a traffic light at an intersection nearby where speeding cars consistently failed to yield right-of-way to pedestrians and where several children had been injured in a short period of time. Now, as such things go, a traffic light is a relatively noncontroversial object; so I had no qualms about authorizing the citizen group sponsoring the demonstration to use the church's name as a supporting agency. (After all, I did not want to be upstaged by the neighborhood Catholic parish also listed as a sponsor!)

On the morning of the demonstration, the captain of the local police precinct came to see me. He asked that I call off the march. I was absolutely flabbergasted. I told him I had no such authority and would not use it even if I did, for I supported the cause the march was intended to dramatize. Why, I asked, had he come to see me instead of someone else whose name might be on the list. He responded that he knew that, being a minister, I would be a "reasonable" man. Furthermore, he continued, the church and the police have the same objective in society. That both intrigued and mystified me, so I asked for an explanation. "Well," he said, "both the church and the police are committed to the preservation of the status quo."

I am not being irreverent when I say, "God, I hope not."

Jesus, "the king of the Jews," has been raised from the dead and now, we say in faith, he is Lord of everything. He is now everybody's king. He is hard at work establishing that kingdom on earth. Oh, to be sure, one way of looking at it would be to say that his kingdom has already come. Yet, one can also say that it is still to come. One thing is certain: It is a real kingdom, one to which the familiar sovereignties of this earth—the United States, France, the Soviet Union, China, and 150 or so others—become subordinate as knees are bent here and there and tongues confess Christ as Lord. Do not blame me if the language offends you; I did not invent it but received it as part of the inheritance I have from brothers and sisters in the faith.

That kingdom which is breaking into the present from the future requires re-interpretation of the past. How pretentious it makes the claims of earthly powers! The sun now never *rises* on the British Empire. The Nazi Third Reich in Germany which, it was boasted by its demonic leaders, would last for a thousand years barely made it for twenty-five. Fifty million Frenchmen have often been proved wrong. Despite the national jingoism over the Panama Canal, who among us is so confident anymore of the Manifest Destiny of our own nation? There is one kingdom which is eternal. It is taking shape in our midst and before our eyes. We can delay its coming, but we cannot stop it.

What good news it is to the monetarily poor and to the poor in spirit that a new kingdom is being established—one that will bring relief from all oppression, one in which the lion will lie down with the lamb and the deserts will bloom and tears will be dried and death will be no more. It is not a kingdom, however, only of metaphor; it is a real kingdom.

It is being established on earth. Jesus came in order to save this world, to save it all—you and me, the government of the United States, the multinational corporations, even the Little League! One of our basic problems, it seems to me, is that we still believe the gospel is primarily for us, when actually it is for the world. We somehow think that the church is intended for our benefit, but its mandate is to minister to the world. Jesus came to redeem and restore it all.

Do you believe it? I do, once in a while. Sometimes I like the world just the way it is. Then it is that I know the reality of the police captain's assumption about the church. If we did not want the world to stay the same, would we not resist it more?

Increasingly—maybe it is an inevitable sign of aging—I find myself longing for a new world. One in which no one goes hungry. One in which people love and care enough, laugh and hope enough, and weep and share enough that everyone feels needed and wanted; one in which energy now siphoned off in protecting ourselves can be channeled into praising the God who was in Christ reconciling the world to himself.

So I allow myself to indulge in still another fantasy. Suppose that politics and the "world" are not synonymous, as many believe? Suppose the political order is up for grabs and that whoever controls it may either make it captive to the kingdoms of this world or to the kingdom of our Lord?

Suppose that, as we energetically and zealously recruited our finest youth to be missionaries a hundred years ago, we were now energetically and zealously to recruit our finest, most sensitive, most brilliant youth to go into government as disciples of Jesus? (Do you know who is doing it? The Moonies are! It is a calculated policy of the Unification Church to get their smartest adherents into leadership positions where they can effect important decisions. I do not want to entrust my future solely to them!)

Suppose that we organized "support groups" in our churches—small groups of conscientious and faithful people who would covenant with these young men and women to be with them through the lonely decisions they have to make, helping them identify the moral issues, helping them see what options are open, helping them to seek the will of the Lord through rigorous thought as well as fervent prayer. While we are at it, suppose we developed the same kind of network for others who have to make responsible use of power in this world.

Suppose we did that. Would it make a difference? Might the kingdom of our Lord come a little faster? I do not know, but I am eager to find out! Jesus' "style" as king seems to sidestep headlong confrontation with the powers of this world (except for very direct confrontation with the forces of organized religion); he appears to have much respect for the ruthlessness with which the "worldly" use their instruments of power. In addition, however, he has confidence in the power of God's Spirit to heal, to restore, to reconcile, to transform, to overcome. On this side of Easter, it is possible for us to have that kind of confidence, too.

The question I would have you ponder, then, is this: "What if Jesus is Lord of the government as well as of the church?"

To retell the stories with which we have been preoccupied in this chapter would be to leave the total story incomplete. So "hear" through your eyes another event involving that extraordinary city of Jerusalem:

That same day two of Jesus' followers were on their way to the village of Emmaus, about seven miles from Jerusalem, and they were talking together earnestly about all these happenings. As they talked and discussed with one another, Jesus himself drew near and walked along with them; but something kept them from recognizing him. He asked, "What is it you are talking about so intently?"

They stopped in their tracks, their faces full of gloom; and one, whose name was Cleopas, answered, "Are you the only person in Jerusalem who does not know the things which have been happening there the past few days?"

"What things?" he asked.

"All the things concerning Jesus of Nazareth, who was a prophet mighty in word and deed before God and all the people, and how our chief priests and rulers handed him over to be sentenced to death and had him crucified. We did so hope that he would be the one to redeem Israel! And now it has been three days since this has happened, and some of the women in our group have astonished us. They went to the tomb early this morning but failed to find his body, and they returned with a story of a vision of angels who told them that he was alive. So some of the men went to check it out and found it was just as the women had said, but him they did not see."

"O foolish men and slow of heart to believe all the prophets have said!" Jesus answered. "Was the Messiah not bound to suffer before entering into his glory?" And beginning with Moses and the prophets, he explained to them all the passages in the Scriptures which referred to himself.

By then they had reached the village to which they were going, and he gave evidence that he intended to continue on further. But they constrained him, saying, "Stay with us, for evening is coming and the day is almost over." So he went in with them. And later, at supper, he took bread and blessed it, broke it, and gave it to them. Then their eyes were opened, and they recognized him; and immediately he vanished from their sight. And they said to one another, "Did not our hearts burn within us as he talked with us on the road and explained the Scriptures to us?"

And immediately they got to their feet and began walking back to Jerusalem. There they found the Eleven and those who were with them, who told them, "The Lord has risen, indeed; he has appeared to Simon Peter." And they told what things had happened to them, and how he had been made known to them in the breaking of bread.

Notes

[1]W. F. Slater, ed., *Matthew,* The Century Bible (London: The Caxton Publishing Co., n.d.), p.231.

[2]A. W. Argyle, *The Gospel According to Matthew,* The Cambridge Bible Commentary on the New English Bible (Cambridge, England: The Syndics of the Cambridge University Press, 1963), p.125.

[3]J. Newton Davies, "Matthew," *Abingdon Bible Commentary* (Nashville: Abingdon Press, 1929), p. 980.

[4]Midrash, Yalkut Shimoni, i, 766 on Numbers 23:9.

[5]James Barr, "Messiah," in *Dictionary of the Bible,* ed. James Hastings (New York: Charles Scribner's Sons, 1963), p. 654.

[6]Albert Schweitzer, *The Quest of the Historical Jesus* (New York: Macmillan Publishing Co., Inc., 1961), p. 403.

[7]Raymond E. Brown, *The Anchor Bible: The Gospel According to John (i-xii)* (Garden City, N.Y.: Doubleday & Co., Inc., 1966), p.233.

[8]Evelyn Underhill, *Collected Papers* (London: Longman's, Green & Co., n.d.), p. 212.

[9]William Temple, *Readings in St. John's Gospel* (London: Macmillan & Co., Ltd., 1959), p. 76.

[10]A. M. Hunter, *The Gospel According to John,* The Cambridge Bible Commentary on the New English Bible (Cambridge, England: The Syndics of the Cambridge University Press, 1965), p.67.

[11]Temple, *op. cit.,* p.102.

[12]Carl Jung, *Modern Man in Search of a Soul* (New York: Harcourt Brace Jovanovich, Inc., 1939), p. 252.

[13]A. M. Hunter, *The Gospel According to Saint Mark,* Torch Bible Commentary (London: SCM Press Ltd., 1949), p. 81.

[14]Charles W. Colson, *Born Again* (Old Tappan, N.J.: Fleming H. Revell Co., Spire Books, 1977), pp. 108-117.

[15]Lloyd Douglas, *The Mirror,* The American Pulpit Series, book 2 (Nashville: Abingdon Press, 1945), p.74.

[16]Brown, *op. cit.,* p.458.

[17]Johann Heerman, stanza a of "Ah Holy Jesu, How Hast Thou Offended," trans. Robert Bridges, *Yattendon Hymnal* (London: Oxford University Press, n.d.). Used by permission of Oxford University Press.